THE TWO MOORS WAY

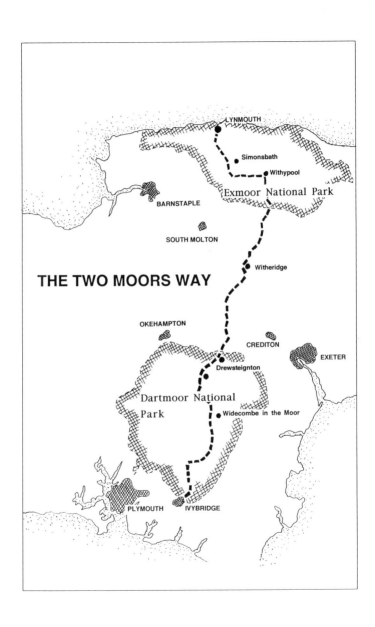

THE TWO MOORS WAY

by

James Roberts

CICERONE PRESS
MILNTHORPE, CUMBRIA

© James Roberts 1994
ISBN 1 85284 159 1
A catalogue record for this book is available from the British Library.

Acknowledgements

My thanks are due to the my wife Elena for her support during the researching and writing of this book. I would also like to thank Walt Unsworth. Thanks are owed to John Earle for his excellent *Walking on Dartmoor*, also published by Cicerone. I owe thanks to Jim Foster, and especially to Dan Fabian for his help with research. Any errors in the text are mine alone.

Advice to Readers

Readers are advised that whilst every effort is taken by the author to ensure the accuracy of this guidebook, changes can occur which may affect the contents. It is advisable to check locally on transport, accommodation, shops etc but even rights-of-way can be altered and, more especially overseas, paths can be eradicated by landslip, forest fires or changes of ownership.

The publisher would welcome notes of any such changes

Front Cover: A scene near Withypool   (Photo: Walt Unsworth)

CONTENTS

The clapper bridge upstream of Huntingdon Cross (see p16)

Chapter One
WALKING THE TWO MOORS WAY

The Two Moors Way has been in existence since 1976; it is a product of cooperation between Devon Ramblers Association and Devon County Council. It is not a National Trail in the way that the South West Coast Path is. Nevertheless, for much of its length it is extremely well waymarked - to the same standard as more famous long-distance paths. In the year of writing this guide the local government officer who was concerned with the Two Moors Way at its outset made a farewell journey along the Way to mark his retirement. However, this was in the county council limousine (registration number DCC 1!), visiting each of the datestones along the route - perhaps the most unusual way of covering the Two Moors Way!

The Two Moors Way runs for approximately 100 miles, from the southern edge of Dartmoor to the spectacular north Devon coastline at Lynmouth. It is a challenging walk involving, at either end, some remote walking across wild moorland. Approximately one half of its length runs across the gentle hill country of mid-Devon - after two days of tight fields of pasture, copses and hedges, you return to the high moorland for the walk's spectacular climax high above the Bristol channel with views across to the mountains of Wales. Most walkers will probably finish the Two Moors Way in five days, if not distracted en route. However there is a wealth of distraction along (and just off) the way and I have laid out the subsequent chapters as six days of walking.

The walker will find that it is not necessary to read this book for every step of the way in order to follow the path.

Initially the book should be used to mark the alignment of the route on the 1:50,000 map, for although it is named on the map it is often not obvious what the exact route of the path is. If you do lose the route, or find it difficult to follow along the intricate network of paths through the tight countryside of mid-Devon, you should find the directions of added help when the map is failing.

Undoubtedly the best maps to use for the walk are the Ordnance Survey 1:50,000 Landranger series. If ever "the map" is referred to without a scale in the subsequent text, it refers to these rather than the 1:25,000 sheets. Dartmoor is covered by a single sheet Outdoor Leisure map at 1:25 000. The sheet is printed on both sides and is an impressive piece of mapping, including every field-boundary. As has been said before, if maps were to show any more information than this, they would be an invasion of privacy! The superb accuracy of survey and sharp printing are somewhat let down by latter-day overprinting with stretches of countryside having "pony trekking" or "forest walks" emblazoned across them. Nevertheless, notwithstanding my disapproval of 1:25,000 maps because they need such frequent extraction from the map-case and re-folding, this is the map that I recommend for the Dartmoor section. The major advantage over the 1:50,000 series is that the actual line of the Two Moors Way, where relevant, is shown. The 1:50,000 sheets you will need to walk the route are Landranger numbers 202, 191, 181 and 180.

The necessity of showing the continuous line of the path on the map is not needed because, once on the open moor, the legal restriction to follow a designated right of way does not exist. Hand in hand with the praiseworthy lack of interfering waymarks on the moor is the principle of "Access Land". The edge of this is clearly marked on the Outdoor Leisure map, by a purple line; "Access Land" applies to unenclosed moorland and some isolated patches of common land on the margins of the moor. Comparing the map to the ground (which you tend to do very frequently whilst walking the Two Moors Way) you can see that the purple Access Land boundary follows the edge of the unreclaimed moor; there can be few instances where a boundary marked on the map is so delightfully and obviously shown on the ground.

The Two Moors Way starts and finishes at towns without a railway station, although both have had stations in the past. There are various different ways of reaching the start and finish of the route. Ivybridge is reached by buses from Plymouth. Lynmouth and Lynton are served by buses from Barnstaple, which is at the terminus of the branch line from Exeter. It is possible to leave your car in Lynmouth and take the bus to Barnstaple, followed by train to Plymouth, changing at Exeter and then catch the bus from Plymouth to Ivybridge - a journey that will take you much of a day. An easier but more expensive option is to park your car at Lynmouth and take a taxi to Ivybridge. A third possibility is to leave your car at the Morchard Road halt and travel to Plymouth by train. Morchard Road is forty minutes by train from Barnstaple and can easily be reached from Lynmouth at the end of the walk; there is parking here for about four cars only on a patch of gravel. There are buses from Lynton to Barnstaple on Sundays, although you need to be in Lynmouth by the middle of the day. They are operated by Red Bus; see Appendix B.

Something that does not yet exist is a link route from the South Devon coast path, up the River Erme from Erme Mouth to Ivybridge, so that the Two Moors Way can be walked as a true coast to coast route. Routes do exist along either bank of the Erme Estuary, although these are not designated rights of way. In this way the walker could head east out of Plymouth (aided by a town bus to Plymstock or perhaps Yealmpton) and follow the South Devon Coast Path east, linking to start the Two Moors Way at Ivybridge. The snag here is that the ferry across the mouth of the Yealm at Newton Ferrers has ceased operating. If you have a week to spare, including the weekends at either end, a wonderful finale to the Two Moors Way would be a three day walk along the North Devon Coast Path to Barnstaple from Lynmouth. The wildest stretch is over by the time you reach Combe Martin, fifteen miles' walk from Lynmouth. The Red Bus Company (see Appendix B) runs buses from Combe Martin and Ilfracombe to Barnstaple. Alternatively a walk due south suggests itself, following the path south and south-west from Great Hangman (GR601480), thence up the track past Yellaton (GR597449) and from there due south over Mattocks Down and down the road to Clifton, followed by the path and road to Arlington. From Arlington church the path heads south-west, crosses the River Yeo (GR606399) into Woolley Wood and follows the west bank of the river, then south-west to Shirwell (GR5937). South from Shirwell the bridleway takes you into the woods along the Yeo, briefly along the road and then left off it (at GR592356) to follow the footpath to Kingdon Gardens and thence into Barnstaple.

As well as providing a worthy challenge for the long-distance walker, the Two Moors Way is an enriching experience, with its variety of fine landscapes, delightful villages and great wealth of history and prehistory encountered along the route.

You will find that the Two Moors Way has this effect on you by the time you finish; you just do not want to pack up your boots and go home! If you find things have changed from the text, please write to the author, care of the publishers. It only remains for me to hope that every reader will have something of the pleasure walking this route that I have enjoyed.

Chapter Two
IVYBRIDGE TO HOLNE - 13 miles

The first day of the Two Moors Way takes you straight from the town of Ivybridge, steeply uphill onto the moor itself, without any preamble through pastoral countryside. Perhaps the most important feature of Dartmoor National Park is that there are no walkers' signposts or waymarking on the moor itself, and indeed through a tight-knit *bocage* of fields, copses and hedges surrounding the moor itself the waymarking is not all that it might be. (It may quite justifiably be argued that waymarking is much more important off the open ground of the moor than on it.) The result is, quite simply, that in order to do any walking across Dartmoor, you have to have a certain competence with a map. There is no more delightful way of improving map reading skills than by following the Two Moors Way.

If you need to park you car at the end of the day's walk, in Scorriton, there is a useful patch of common land where cars can be parked, saving the walk uphill from the village, at GR694685.

The Two Moors Way may be considered to start outside the Bridge Inn in the centre of Ivybridge, where the old main Exeter to Plymouth main road crosses the River Erme. Turning right out of the Bridge Inn, follow Harford Road northwards along the east bank of the River Erme, climbing steeply up the hill away from the town centre. You pass Stowford paper mill and follow the narrow lane up past the secondary school on the right. At the road junction at GR641568 (marked on the map as a T-junction, though now become a crossroads with the recent building of a small housing estate on the left) you find a green plaque confirming that you are entering Dartmoor

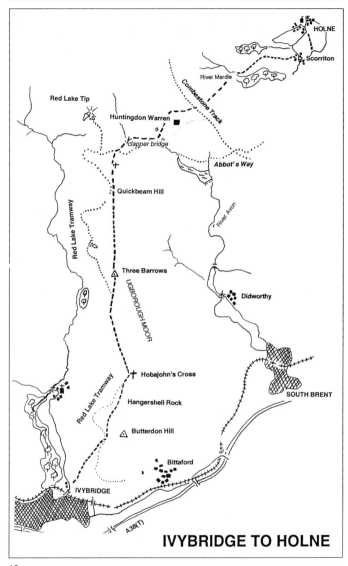

IVYBRIDGE TO HOLNE

National Park. There is also a stone here commemorating the opening of the Two Moors Way in 1976. (Henceforward the Two Moors Way will simply be referred to as the "Way".) Continue north-east up Harford Road, over the railway at Stowford Bridge. 300 yards after crossing the railway, turn right opposite Stowford House, a signpost telling you that this is the "bridlepath to the moor". Almost immediately you turn left, to head north-east up a green lane between high hedges; it ends at a wooden gate leading on to the moor.

This is a point of wonderful anticipation of delights to come; within a mile of starting the Way you are out on the open vastness of Dartmoor. Ahead of you on the horizon are the cairns on the summits of Butterdon Hill and Weatherdon Hill. There is a barely perceptible col between them; head towards this, a fine path leading across sheep-cropped turf between the bracken. The line of beech trees and stone wall, marking the edge of the open moor, falls away to your left and every step brings wider views of South Devon behind you. Half a mile after leaving the farm lane you look down to your left to see the romantic ivy-clad ruin of Addicombe (GR647582). A few steps further and, at a barely-perceptible cairn in the bracken you meet the old tramway - a well defined route snaking up onto the high moor.

Cross the tramway here, continuing to head north, between the cairns of Wetherdon Hill and Butterdon Hill. As you reach the top of the hill you see the prominent crag of Hangershell Rock ahead. Make for this and from there head just east of north to join the tramway again. Follow the tramway along the western flank of Ugborough Moor with views of the great spoil heaps of the extensive china clay diggings west and north of the village of Cornwood.

The tramway that is a major feature of this morning's walk was completed in 1912; it carried men and equipment up from Cantrell, near Bittaford, just to the east of Ivybridge, a total of just over 8 miles to the China Clay works at Redlake, on the southern flanks of Green Hill. Later in the day the Way passes well within sight of the old clay diggings. The produce of the workings was carried down in pipes as a liquid emulsion. The workings and tramway closed in 1932. Between Glasscombe Ball and Ugborough Moor it offers the best route northwards, and on a day of bad weather it is worth following all the way to within a mile of its terminus. However, in fine weather, a much more rewarding walk can be had by turning right off the tramway as it skirts Three Barrows Hill (GR 653626) on its western flank. The view from the top is simply superb; to your left you look clear down into Plymouth Sound - a vivid reminder of heroic deeds during the battles of the Spanish Armada in 1588. Ahead, the vast expanse of Dartmoor is spread before you; the high masts which are such a prominent landmark are located on North Hessary Tor, just behind Princetown. Behind you and to your right are views of Lyme Bay beyond Torbay and Dartmouth; on occasion I have been able to look at the lighthouse on Portland Bill through binoculars from here. The three enormous barrows of grey, weathered granite on top of the hill, mark the summit of Harford Moor; from various points along the way as you make your way towards the summit you can see the square tower of Harford village church (worth a detour off the Two Moors Way in itself). In the church belfry are four slate memorials on the wall, commemorating the villagers who served in the time of the Armada, sailing no doubt from Plymouth sound, at the furthest edge of the view to the west from Three Barrows.

Looking northwards from the trig point you can follow the line of the tramway as it heads away to the north and swings to the left through the prominent line of old boundary stones just before the old clay pit at Left Lake Mires and contours round Quickbeam Hill. In bad visibility this is no doubt the easiest route to follow, as far as the ruin just to the west of Crossways (GR647659). For the stretch as far as a point half a mile beyond Left Lake Mires the tramway follows a course parallel to the much earlier Blackwood Path. This can be followed on the map, from Wrangaton Cross (GR678581) all the way north to one of the finest cattle pounds on Dartmoor, Erme Pound (GR630655), where the right of way is marked as ending. In fact there is a more direct and much more interesting route, heading almost exactly due north down the hill from the northernmost of the three barrows. You can see the path, faint but quite followable, heading away to the north, following a prominent line of ancient boundary stones just to the west of the small pool on the southern flanks of Quickbeam Hill (GR656645). For many centuries now, these boundary stones have indicated the limits of the parish of Harford, however there can be no doubt that the stones predate the English settlement of Harford, first recorded in the Domesday Book. Incidentally, the name Harford has the same origin as the cathedral city of Hereford in the Welsh borders, and the large town of Herford in Germany. It means the ford of the "Here" or army. The path follows the line of the boundary stones northwards. Just to the right of the direction you are heading in you see the unusual turret-shaped cairn of Eastern White Barrow (GR666652) - a useful landmark.

The path takes you just to the west of Petre's Pits, site of the attempted china clay workings at the head of the Bala Brook. These are marked on the 1:50,000 map at GR659648 but are not named. For the final part of the climb to Petre's Cross you are on the old Zeal Tor Tramway (alternatively known as the Shipley Track), a much earlier and now less obvious route than the Red Lake tramway. It dates from 1847 and was initially constructed to carry the produce of the attempt at naphtha extraction just south of Red Lake. It lasted just three years although it was briefly reactivated to carry the produce from Petre's Pits, mentioned above, down to Shipley Bridge on the River Avon.

Petre's Cross marks the remotest point reached on Dartmoor on the Way. Directly ahead is the prominent landmark of the conical pyramid of the "sky tip" - the old spoil heap of Red Lake China Clay works. At Petre's Cross the stones from the Bronze Age Cairn were used to build a shelter by the men working at the Red Lake pits; though roofless it still offers shelter from the wind. The cross (GR6960), erected as a boundary marker for Sir William Petre (then Lord of the Manor of Brent) was broken up and used as a lintel; the stem of the cross has now been replaced in an upright position (apparently upside down!), minus the arms. The cross marked the boundary between the manor of Brent and the Royal Forest of Dartmoor and is on the route of the Perambulation of the year 1240 when twelve knights drew up the boundary. In fact the Way only just touches the Royal Forest of Dartmoor, the boundary of which runs up the Western Wella Brook past Huntingdon Warren. Less than an hour is spent walking in the old Royal Forest itself, before you exit from it by crossing the Western Wella Brook near Huntingdon Warren.

Beyond Petre's Cross the Way is less well marked on the ground. From Petre's Cross head north, down the hill towards the old spoil heap for 400 yards. It brings you past the flat roofed blowing house, marked on the map at GR652651, to the grassy track of the Abbot's Way. This leaves the old tramway by the ruin just to the west of Crossways at GR647659. Follow the Abbot's Way due east from here, down towards the valley of the Avon. The best spot to cross the Avon is the delightful clapper bridge at GR657662; a path descends steeply down a bank, directly to it. Ahead of you are the prominent ancient field boundaries on the south side of Huntingdon Warren. The Abbot's Way proper follows the south bank of the Avon to ford it by the remains of what seems to be an old footbridge at its confluence with the western Wella Brook.

From the ancient clapper bridge the route lies on the north side of the Avon, undefined but a pleasant walk across heather, bracken and grass to the old fields surrounding the now disappeared Huntingdon Warren Farm. As you approach the site of the former farm you can see the Abbot's Way, well defined, heading down the Avon Valley past Bishop's Meads, then to head east across Dean burn before descending to cross the Dean Burn at a very fine clapper bridge in the woods.

All that remains of Huntingdon Warren now is a fine old sycamore tree on the uphill side of the fields, marking the site of the house. The warren (purpose-built rabbit colony) was worked for most of the nineteenth century and the house was inhabited until 1956. Cross the delightful Western Wella Brook (if it is in spate there is a footbridge just upstream of the fields at GR667671.) Just downstream on the south bank is the obvious ruin of the Revd Keble Martin's chapel. He was the author of *Concise British Flora in Colour;* the chapel was built by him and a group of kindred spirits in the early years of the twentieth century. In 1990 he was commemorated at a wedding held on the spot, attended by fellow hikers on the moor. From the footbridge across the Western Wella brook the Way runs east, following the clearly defined Huntingdon Warren track past the obvious ruin of the wheelpit of the old Huntingdon tin mine on the right.

The Huntingdon Warren Track runs east from here, an obvious grassy track across the bracken-covered hillside, bringing you to the hilltop track junction at GR675671. This is the junction of the Huntingdon Warren Track with the Combestone Track, a much longer route running north from the village of South Brent (GR6960) via Gidley Bridge (GR703638) then north-west to where you are standing. It then goes over the summit of Pupers Hill, Hapstead Ford across the nascent River Mardle (GR671693) and Holne Ridge to cross Sandy Way and head north, down to Horn's Cross (GR669712) and Combestone Tor, to descend to cross the River Dart at Week Ford, finishing at Huccaby (GR660729).

From the junction there are fine views eastwards across the slopes of Buckfastleigh Moor and all the way to the sea beyond Torbay - having made its way up onto Dartmoor by its southern tip, the Way now descends off its eastern flank. As you descend along the way to Lud Gate you need to turn left off the track shortly after the junction to head north-east, again the route being named on the map although it is not marked. The way is all the more delightful for there being no obvious path on the ground - long may it stay this way! Ahead of you is the obvious line of trees marking the track from Chalk Ford to Scorriton. You descend steeply, the hillside scattered with thorn trees, to cross the River Mardle by a wooden footbridge at Chalk Ford. On the far bank you go through a gate with a signpost ("Scorriton 1^1/$_2$ miles") and join a farm track heading east and skirting the southern edge of Scorriton Down. To the left the field is fenced high to keep in a flock of domesticated red deer. The track becomes an enclosed farm lane as you head east, away from the open moor and down to the village of Scorriton. On the descent to the village there is a useful patch of common land where cars can be parked at GR694685. For the last part of the descent to the village, you are descending along a spur between the valley of the Holy Brook to your left and the River Mardle to your right; both of these are tributaries of the River Dart. The ever-widening farm lane takes you straight to the centre of Scorriton.

On reaching the road junction in the village turn left to

find the Tradesmen's Arms, a welcoming pub with a children's play room and serving good food. There is no shop in Scorriton nor even a church; the War Memorial, no more than a plaque on a wall, commemorates the men of "West Buckfastleigh" parish who fell in the First World War. It is an extra delight that this tiny village, not even a parish in its own right, supports a good pub.

The walk to Holne does not appear to be waymarked, although it is easy to follow. Turn left out of the Tradesmen's Arms and immediately left again in the centre of the village. You head down the hill, out of the village, keeping left at a minor road junction (GR707686). Immediately after the bridge turn left up a sunken stony farm lane "unsuitable for motors" to head up the hill, joining the tarred lane again just before Play Cross (GR705694). On the way up the lane there are fine views through a couple of gateways on the left, up the valley of the Holy Brook to the west.

The village of Holne is a delightful spot to end the day. It has all the walker could wish for - delightful old buildings, a well-stocked and friendly shop, a fine and ancient pub where you can stay and plenty of households offering bed and breakfast and some camping too (see Appendix A). Before exploring the village itself, the long walk across the moor from Ivybridge surely merits the first Devon Cream tea of the Two Moors Way, outside on the patio at The Old Forge Tearooms.

Between the tearooms and the pub is the fourteenth-century church of St Mary. Inside there is a fine carved pulpit, as well as painted roof-bosses in the chancel, superb ceiling work and an unusual screen made up of some forty panels. A former incumbent of Holne was the Revd Kingsley, father of Charles Kingsley, the author of *The Water Babies*. He was born at the vicarage in 1819 and no doubt in his childhood knew the ancient, entirely hollow yew tree in the churchyard.

Many such have been proved to be much older than their adjacent churches. Holne itself is first recorded in the Domesday Book, its name simply meaning "holly". At that time there were some twenty families recorded as living in the parish.

THE ABBOT'S WAY

For a brief section in the latter part of the day the Two Moors Way follows the Abbot's Way along the Avon Valley. This is the first of a number of such ancient trackways encountered on the walk.

The Abbot's Way takes its name from the fact that it connects the ancient abbeys of Buckfast and Tavistock and perhaps Buckland as well. However it is not known exactly when it was so named. In the west, Buckfast Abbey, unusually for monastic foundations in England, pre-dates the Norman Conquest, having been founded in the year 1018 in the reign of the Danish King Canute. On the western side of the moor, Buckland was founded more than two centuries later, around 1280. Tavistock Abbey, of which almost nothing now remains, predates the other two, having been founded in 974 and for almost all of its history until the Dissolution in 1539 was the most important monastic centre, even owning its own private port at Morewellham Quay, on the Tamar, from where Dartmoor wool and tin was exported and lime fertiliser imported.

The original alignment of the way ran west over Hockmoor from Buckfast Abbey to cross the River Mardle at GR724675. Of the three abbeys, Buckfast is now the only one where you will find any monks, having been rebuilt in 1907 by French Benedictines, who completed the rebuilding of the church in 1938. From the crossing of the River Mardle the way headed just south of west to Cross Furzes, nowadays the finish of the public road. From here it headed up to Water Oak Corner

The valley of the River Mardle near Scorriton

(GR685660) and over the moor to follow the Avon upstream
to Huntingdon Cross, below Huntingdon Warren ruin,
described above. Thence it ran due west, then north-west,
past Erme Head and Cist Cairn (GR612680) on the western
slopes of Great Gnats' Head to Nun's (or Siward's) cross. It
would seem that the Buckland Abbey version headed west
from Broad Rock, the col above Erme Head, towards Sheepstor
and so to Buckland Abbey. From Nunn's Cross it ran directly,
just west of north to Princetown, from where its course to
Tavistock is now followed by the modern main road.

The Abbot's Way offers a tempting diversion for the
walker along the Two Moors Way, from Huntingdon Cross
to Buckfast and Buckfastleigh, three miles to the east. If you
are so tempted, there is an attractive return route, re-uniting
with the Two Moors Way at Holne. It diverts from the
Scorriton road at the junction with the farm lane at GR723677
and follows the farm track and then bridleway into Burchetts

Wood from there, down to the Holy Brook to follow it upstream to cross it at Mill Leat Bridge (GR714685). From here you follow the footpath upstream along the northern bank of the brook to join the public road, where you turn left, past Langaford Farm. If you turn right to follow the footpath through the farm you rejoin the Two Moors Way (GR707687) on its way up the stony track to Holne.

There is a lot of evidence to show that the Abbot's Way came about by monks following pre-existing trackways across the moor, rather than creating the route for themselves. There are few crosses on the route and, interestingly, one of them - Nun's Cross - was previously known as Siward's Cross. One may speculate that it was renamed in honour of the nuns passing this way to and from the abbeys. However it came about, the stretch of the Abbot's Way that runs for some 12 miles (19km) from Buckfast to Princetown is a fascinating and delightful moorland walk in its own right.

Chapter Three
HOLNE TO CHAGFORD - 18 miles

This is a superb day's walk. A tribute to the creators of the Two Moors Way is due, for instead of cutting straight across the heart of the Moor itself, the path takes in a great variety of scenery as it makes its way northwards across Dartmoor's eastern marches, with views across the open moors and the gentler country of east Devon. The walking varies from moorland to farm lanes and paths.

From the porch at the front of the Church House Inn in the centre of the village, turn left and head straight across at the staggered crossroads immediately in front of you. Make your way north-east along the narrow lane for 300 yards which brings you to the T-junction at Butts Cross. Turn left here for 100 yards along the road, before turning right over a stile. The path, fenced in at first, heads north down the hill and over a couple of stiles before joining an ancient green lane just before Cleave Wood. This old lane leads for 1/2 mile along the south bank of the River Dart downstream through the National Trust property of Holne Woods, past Horseshoe Falls to meet the public road at New Bridge. Turn left on the road here.

Across the river there is a car park and a National Park information office. The National Park office has a good selection of books and sells all Ordnance Survey maps of the area. The staff working here are a mine of information, which tends to be more willingly offered at the less busy times when they are not besieged by car-borne hordes. During the summer you can normally be assured of finding an ice cream here from a van. This area is a very popular spot in summer, largely with family groups enjoying the moor and the River

HOLNE TO DOCKWELL CROSS

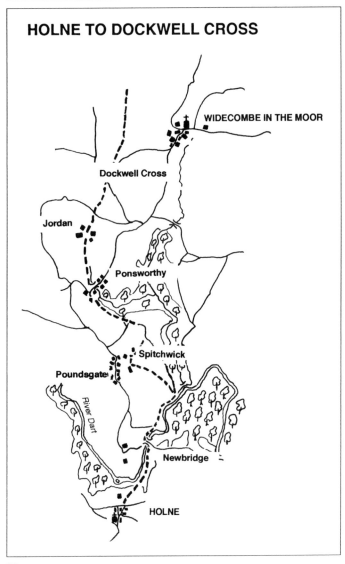

Dart.

In former times the Two Moors Way went steeply up the hill towards Aish Tor and thence along "Doctor Blackall's Drive" to Bel Tor, whence it descended to Ponsworthy. Now it follows a more easterly route through the Webburn Valley. Keep right as you head over the bridge and follow the road round under the trees to the blind junction at Barren Corner (GR713712). Turn right, off the main road here, and follow the unfenced road northwards under the trees down to the flat common land of Deeper Marsh. Along the river bank here grow a number of alder buckthorn, in former times a valuable tree for the use of its charcoal in the manufacture of gunpowder. It is also the food species for the Brimstone butterfly, making the site ecologically important. Deeper Marsh is a popular spot for families with children to spend lazy summer days by the moorland river.

Follow the road northwards through the trees, past the entrance to the drive to Spitchwick Manor at Spitchwick Lower Lodge. There is a sign here pointing to the bed and breakfast at Leigh Tor Farm (see Appendix A). If you do want to stay here, you should follow the Two Moors Way along the road to Townwood Farm (which also offers bed and breakfast and has the added attraction of being on the Two Moors Way itself - see Appendix A). From here head up the hill to the junction with the drive at GR708724, where you turn left and follow the private road to Leigh Tor. This is an attractive area to stay, with the pleasant Tavistock Arms pub in Poundsgate offering good food. More than this, according to tradition, one Sunday in October 1638, Satan paused here before setting forth to ride to Widecombe in order to settle a debt with a certain Jan Reynolds, who had borrowed from him when out of pocket through card playing. This is narrated in a traditional poem, the relevant lines:

The months went by. October came.
At Poundsgate on the hill
Mine hostess took a golden coin
And put it in the till.

'Twas paid her by a handsome guy
Well dressed beyond belief:
That same Old Nick......

If you should stop at the Tavistock Inn for a drink, cast a look around to see if there is any "...handsome guy / Well dressed beyond belief...." The interweaving of fact with legend is fascinating, for the story of Satan dragging poor Jan out of Widecombe church is connected with one of the most ferocious storms ever seen on Dartmoor, which indeed damaged the church, killed four and injured sixty in the village. More prosaically, there is also a campsite in Poundsgate (see Appendix A).

From Spitchwick Lower Lodge follow the road along and turn left at the fork to head up the hill towards Leusdon and Ponsworthy. Turn left off the road as it turns sharply to the right at Townwood Farm (GR717720). Townwood Farm also offers bed and breakfast (see Appendix A). Follow the lane north-west along the gully, through Great Wood. The path bears left by a pond hidden in the trees to the right and heads almost due west across two fields to join the narrow tarred lane leading to Spitchwick Manor. A nineteenth-century incumbent of Spitchwick Manor, one Dr Blackall, was responsible for the track above the Dart Valley from Aish Tor to Mel Tor which now carries his name. It was routed so as to have the best possible views across to the west towards Holne Moor. The Way used to follow the drive but the stretch of the route just before Bel Tor Corner (GR695732) went along a track that was not, apparently, a right of way.

Looking east across the Dart valley from the flanks of Pupers Hill

Just in front of Spitchwick Farm the path turns right off the lane and heads east for a few yards across a field with a garden on the left. At the end of the garden the path swings to the left and heads across two fields to join the road at Lower Town. Turn left on the road and head up the hill, past Leusdon Lodge Hotel, which advertises that it offers tea and coffee to non-residents, although it does not look as though it is the kind of place a booted walker would feel comfortable in. On the right at the top of the hill you reach the church which has served as a landmark for the preceding mile. The Way now follows the tarred public road north-west across the northern edge of Leusdon Common and then, gorse-banked, follows the line of the West Webburn River, flowing through the woods well below it to the right. It drops down past the seventeenth-century farm at Sweaton and reaches the road junction at the ford in the middle of Ponsworthy. The cottages by the ford here are some of the most photographed on Dartmoor; one was formerly the blacksmith's shop, betrayed by its double stable door.

From the ford you may well want to divert down to Ponsworthy Bridge (over which Satan is held to have galloped on his black steed en route from Poundsgate to Widecombe that fateful Sunday afternoon in 1638 alluded to above). From the ford head along the path that takes you due north, along the right-hand side of the cottage and thence for the best part of a mile through the woods to exit from the trees just before crossing the river by Mill House. Turn right on the farm lane and then left onto the public road where, interrupted by a couple of gates, it passes through the farmyard of the picturesque former manor farm at Jordan.

Follow the road up the hill, past Drywell Farm to reach Drywell Cross (GR701754) at the top. Here, set against the wall is a fine old wayside cross, in fact the combination of the original cross head, found incorporated into a wall and the shaft from elsewhere in the county. There is an intriguing tiny niche cut into the face. If you want to reach the youth hostel among the conifer plantations at Bellever, turn left here and follow the road north-west for 4 miles - notice the short cut at West Shallowford Farm. To follow the Way, go straight ahead at the crossroads, down to the delightful old farm of Dockwell. Continue up the hill, past some half-worked blocks of granite on the left-hand side of the road in a paddock, to a sign on the left, indicating the permissive footpath to see the deserted mediaeval settlement at approximately GR702759. At last, at Dockwell Cross, passing through the old gateway, you are on the open moor again. Should you be inclined, the almost world-famous village of Widecombe in the Moor lies a mile to the north-east along the road from Dockwell Cross.

"Two Moors Way undefined" says the map - in fact it could scarcely be easier to follow; the obvious feature on the

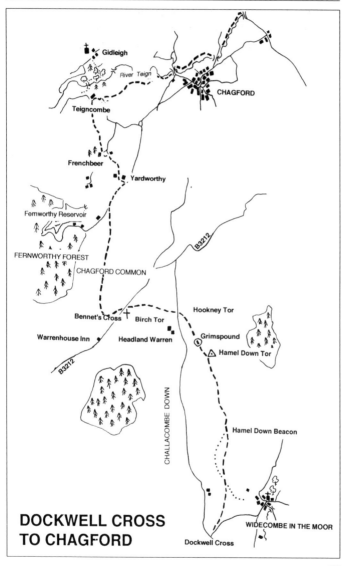

DOCKWELL CROSS TO CHAGFORD

Gidleigh

River Teign

CHAGFORD

Teigncombe

Frenchbeer

Yardworthy

Fernworthy Reservoir

B3212

FERNWORTHY FOREST

CHAGFORD COMMON

Bennet's Cross   Birch Tor   Hookney Tor

Warrenhouse Inn   Headland Warren   Grimspound

Hamel Down Tor

B3212

CHALLACOMBE DOWN

Hamel Down Beacon

WIDECOMBE IN THE MOOR

Dockwell Cross

horizon in front of you is Hamel Down Beacon, 2 miles northwards. To follow the Way, simply wend your way more or less due north to the summit. Although the Way is not marked on the ground there is a slightly incongruous signpost at the edge of the field at GR 706774 indicating the path to Widecombe. On the way to the top are a couple of signboards indicating an alternative path to avoid erosion. In fact the path they are advocating appears to be more eroded than the one they are trying to avoid.

From the summit of Hamel Down Beacon (GR708789) follow the obvious track just west of north, along the fence marking the edge of the reclaimed moorland of Blackaton Down. This is the best viewpoint since Petre's Cross on the preceding day, with fine views across to the west The masts on North Hessary Tor, above Princetown, that seemed so far ahead then are now behind and to the left. It is fast and easy walking here, on a smooth worn track across the heather; this is probably the only spot on the Way where you are likely to see any grouse. There are various stakes dotted around on the moor, dating from the summer of 1940 when they were erected to prevent German troop-carrying gliders landing on the level plateau. Suddenly the memorials in Harford church, passed on the day before, erected in honour of those who fought to prevent a foreign invasion in 1588 seem the more significant.

Just to make everything altogether perfect for the walker, along this stretch, every barrow that is named on the map is also named on the ground, with a series of neat white stones which carry an air of almost military orderliness as well as a sense of the sepulchral. In turn you pass Two Barrows, Single Barrow and Broad Barrow (or "Burrow" as the marker stones would have it). The stones are dated 1854 and were erected on the orders of the Duke of Somerset, marking the boundaries of his estate of Natsworthy Manor (GR720800), just to the east in the valley of the East Webburn River.

At Broad Barrow the path swings to the left to reach Hamel Down Cross. Here the Duke of Somerset's mason made his mark, although he was certainly not responsible for the erection of the cross he nevertheless engraved "H C" (Hamel Cross) and "D S" (Duke of Somerset) - defacing now honoured with antiquity. Here the Way diverges from the Natsworthy Manor boundary, which heads north-east from here, past the Grey Weather stone to the Blue Jug stone, marking the source of the East Webburn River. Leaving Hamel Cross head just west of north to the cairn on the summit of Hamel Down Tor. From this fine vantage point the eye is drawn north, right across the intricate farming country of mid Devon that we are to walk across for the next two days, before reaching the barely perceptible line of the high ground of Exmoor on the far horizon. There are a few rock slabs here, offering a perfect natural platform whereon to sit and admire the view. The rest of the day's walk can be discerned to the north-west, across the summit of Birch Tor. Beyond this can be seen the tops of the trees of Fernworthy Forest and beyond this still the cairn on the summit of Hangingstones Hill. Further to the right you can make out Castle Drogo, which we pass on the following day. This is one of the finest viewpoints on the Way, and, sadly it is something of a farewell to Dartmoor, for there is just a couple of hours of walking left on the Moor itself.

Below, to the right is the saddle in front of King Tor and the obvious track heading west, down the gully to cross the enclosure at Grimspound. Head north-west, steeply down the well worn path to the prehistoric enclosure and cross the tiny trickle of the Grimslake stream.

Grimspound is one of the best known prehistoric sites on Dartmoor. Its name is Anglo Saxon and is one of many that attribute prehistoric features to Grimm - Grimm being a synonym for Woden or Odin. Comparisons may be made with Grime's Graves, the flint mines in Suffolk, or Grim's Ditch in Wiltshire. It is generally thought that Grimspound dates from the early Bronze Age. It is not a fortification against human marauders but against the wild beasts of the moor, which then included the full European panoply of bears, wolves and so on. One of its best features is the entrance, stone paved to prevent it being clogged with mud. It encloses around four acres of moorland.

From Grimspound you have the choice of heading over the summit of Hookney Tor, its flanks pocked with old tin-workings, or else following the path that contours around its western side, looking down at Headland Warren Farm, in days gone by the Birch Tor Inn serving the local miners. Whichever of these paths you take, they bring you to the lonely Challacombe Down road. This is crossed by an ancient trackway from Shapley (GR7082) to Bennet's Cross at GR 695816. This is just to the north of the point where the road crosses the saddle between the bowl of East Bovey Head to the north and the head of the West Webburn to the south. Follow the well-trodden path due west here, over the summit of Birch Tor and then down to the road at Bennet's Cross, the ground to the left as you descend pockmarked with old mine workings of the Birch Tor and Vitifer mines.

On the southern flank of Birch Tor are four fields, known traditionally as the "Four Aces". When Satan caught up with Jan Reynolds in his pew in Widecombe Church (for explanation see above) he found him with his playing cards beside him. Snatching him up and flying up into the air (in the process knocking down masonry to kill four of the congregation) he set off to the west across the moor. The four aces fell out of poor Jan Reynolds grasp and spun to the ground where they lie to this day - or so the story goes. If you do walk over the southern flank of Birch Tor you can follow the track that runs from Headland Warren Farm due west to meet the road by the welcoming Warren House Inn - altogether a very attractive idea.

The Two Moors Way crosses the main B3212 Moretonhampstead to Princetown road at Bennet's cross, now a stump standing a few yards to the east of the road. Tantalisingly, there is no sign on the map of the alignment of the route as it heads more or less north along the spur of Chagford Common, between the gullies of the North Walla Brook and the Metherall Brook. Head south-west from Bennet's Cross, picking up a narrow cutting, part of the old mine workings at Bushdown. Follow this around the head of the North Walla Brook as it swings around to the right and up on to the ridge of Chagford Common. Away to the left the Hurston Row, one of the longest stone rows on Dartmoor, heads away almost due north towards the Heath Stone. You walk past the evidence of some Bronze Age settlement, where a fine cremation urn was found, now exhibited in Plymouth museum. Shortly afterwards you pass the remains of Western Vitifer mine down on the right. The descent to the Fernworthy road makes for fast walking; this is the last stretch on Dartmoor of the Two Moors Way.

Follow the road to Chagford to the left-hand turning down the lane to Yardworthy Farm (GR681850). You are now walking along the Mariners' Way, a brief description of which is given below. Head north down the hill from the farm buildings at Yardworthy - one of the oldest farms in the area. Along this stretch you make your way through two antique gateways still used according to their original design, with horizontal poles placed in sockets in the upright granite posts. Just before the bottom you bear left to cross the South Teign River on a footbridge hidden among the trees. Heading north-west you climb steeply up the hill with a hedge on your left, bringing you up to the hotel at Teignworthy. Turn left by the entrance to the hotel to head along a very narrow walled-in track which almost immediately turns sharply to the right to cross the public road at Great Frenchbeer. Head north from here, initially on a track which deteriorates to a footpath as you make your way along the east-facing slopes of Kes Tor with fine views down into the valley of the South Teign. Ahead you can see the rather baronial residence of Ford Park above the trees. Crossing the private drive to Boldventure Farm, you make your way across a number of tiny fields and walk through a patch of delightful marshy willow and alder scrub where netting-covered duckboards have been laid. The route through here is well waymarked - it needs to be as it snakes through a wonderfully intricate landscape. You cross a deeply rutted lane under some ancient beech trees as you enter the woods behind Yelfords and exit from them to make your way across two fields to meet the private drive at Teigncombe, where a house has been named in honour of the Mariners' Way beside which it stands.

In fact the eponymous cottage marks the point where the Two Moors Way parts company with the Mariners'. The tiny village of Gidleigh, however, offers a tempting short diversion to the north, notwithstanding the closing of the small youth hostel there. Bear left at the cottage to take the right-hand fork up the hill, a signpost pointing the way. The path turns sharp right along the bottom of a coniferous plantation then joins the tarred road for a few yards. Continuing north it turns right off the road to head down the hill on a track. It drops steeply in the woods to the modern footbridge just upstream of Glassy Steps. The path takes you uphill through the woods to the west of Gidleigh Park Hotel, a steep and rocky path flanking the summit of Gidleigh Tor. Heading north-west down the hill with a coniferous plantation on your left it brings you to the road at Gidleigh; turn right and then left. The church has the Gidleigh leat flowing through the churchyard and adjacent to it, the remains of Gidleigh Castle,

Teigncombe Farm near Chagford

in fact a late Norman fortified house; the ruins are private. The church itself, built of Dartmoor granite, has a fine Tudor rood screen, richly painted. About 100 yards south of the castle is Gidleigh Pound - an enclosure for stray livestock. Unless you want to treat yourself to lunch at the Gidleigh Park Hotel (the owner himself is a keen mountain walker and the walk to the hotel is signed from Gidleigh, although it should be stressed that this is not a public right of way and should only be used if you are visiting the hotel - see Appendix A) and walk down the drive to Leigh Bridge, you should retrace your steps back to Teigncombe to rejoin the Two Moors Way.

At Mariners' Way cottage (GR672871) go down the hill to join the public road heading east down the hill, past the yard of the delightful Teigncombe Farm on the left, which offers bed and breakfast (see Appendix A). 400 yards after Teigncombe Farm, turn left at a sharp right-hand bend into North Hill Lane, past the entrance to the farm of the same

35

name on the left, to follow this narrow byway north-east down the hill to meet the road to Gidleigh Park Hotel by Leigh Bridge. This is a delightful lane, for much of its length almost entirely hidden from the rest of the world by high banks and hedges.

From Leigh Bridge, at the confluence of the North and South Teign, follow the road for ¹/₂ mile east to drop steeply down the hill to Holy Street Manor. Notice the small statue of a bishop, with his mitre and crozier, high up under the gable facing the road. In spite of the ecclesiastical look to the place, and the chapel within dedicated to St Boniface, the name of this manor, dating back to the fifteenth century, appears to have derived not from "holy", but rather "hollow". The name refers to the position of the manor on the tongue of land almost enclosed by a meander in the deep valley of the River Teign. From Holy Street Manor the road takes you twisting under the trees for a short stretch by the river itself. Just before you exit from the trees, notice a sluice on the right, controlling the flow into a mill leat that is the road's companion along the way to Chagford Bridge. Unusually, notwith-standing the mill that it originally served now being disused, the old mill leat is in fine flow still, and with a population of small trout. Occasional gaps through the hedge on the left give enticing views down into the clear stream flowing fast over swaying weed and bright gravel. A little less than ¹/₂ mile after Holy Street Manor you reach Factory Cross, just before Chagford. This commemorates the former woollen mill on the left, now the kennels of the Mid Devon Hunt.

Turn left at Factory Cross to follow the Two Moors Way proper; if you want to walk into Chagford village, keep straight ahead. Chagford Bridge certainly dates from the Tudor era, and quite possibly earlier. The name of the village itself (first mentioned in the Domesday Book) comes from the original ford across the river at this spot. "Chag" is an archaic, dialect name for gorse. The route followed by the Two Moors Way is delightful, through fields and along the banks of the trout-filled Teign; the undoubted charm of the town itself is dulled by the sheer number of visitors to be found there on summer weekends.

Chagford became a small town owing to the importance of the tin mining in the vicinity. It was one of the five stannary towns, where the tin was weighed and stamped. Nowadays its business is visitors. There are a great wealth of services offered here, including a NatWest bank open every day. There are several pubs and teahouses, a bakery, and a fine emporium claiming to sell hardware, but also selling all kinds of gear for the camper and walker, as well as books and maps. In the centre of the market square is the Market House, sometimes known as "The Pepperpot".

THE MARINERS' WAY

The Mariners' Way is an ancient route from the port of Bideford, on Devon's north coast to Dartmouth on the English channel coast. It derives its name from the idea that seamen from these two ports on opposite sides of the West Country peninsula used this route when walking from the one to the other.

What remains to be seen today is a rump of the former coast to coast route - the section across the north-eastern flank of Dartmoor from Widecombe to Sticklepath. The complete route went apparently from Dartmouth north-west to Totnes and Ashburton and thence to Widecombe. From there it ran parallel to the modern Two Moors Way to Lettaford. North of Widecombe its alignment can be followed on the map. From Lettaford it ran north-west to Yardworthy, from where its route to Teigncombe is described above. Continuing to flank the moor itself, it continued to Gidleigh, through Throwligh, Clannaborough and South Zeal to

Sticklepath. Onwards from Sticklepath the exact route northwards down the valleys of the Okement and the Torridge is now lost. Interestingly, the version of the route outlined by John Earle is rather different from the one given here.

The question is - why should an ancient route (that is by its very definition a coast to coast path) now only be evident in a section midway across the peninsula? The obvious answer is that it is just one of a myriad old relics on Dartmoor that remain because of the lack of disturbance of ground on the moor. The problem here is that the route is not on the moor itself, but through farmland. The mystery remains.

The date of the appearance of the way is not known with any certainty. However, all the evidence points to a peak of usage in the middle of the eighteenth century. William Crossing suggests that at this time there would have been rest houses every ten or so miles along the way. The parish records of Gidleigh church mention the giving of alms to sailors between the years 1730 and 1774. The stretch that is followed by the Two Moors Way south of Gidleigh can have changed but little since that time.

Signpost and lichen on the Mariners' Way near Frenchbeer

Chapter Four
CHAGFORD TO MORCHARD BISHOP - 19 miles

This is the first of two days of walking across the intricate farming country of central Devon. You quickly realise that it makes for slower going than the open moorland, with a multitude of gates and stiles, and little chance to develop a steady rhythm of walking as you can on the open moorland at either end of the Two Moors Way. Rain at any time of year can quickly turn cattle-trodden lanes, gateways and field corners into areas of semi-liquid mud. Gaiters, especially the excellent "Yeti" type can be very valuable in this region. It is a day to enjoy the ancient villages and pubs of the area. Each hill top reached brings yet more distant views of Dartmoor behind, until, making your way out of the magnificent Teign Gorge below Castle Drogo, you can see Exmoor beckoning ahead.

Leave Chagford along the Drewsteignton Road as it crosses Rushford Bridge. Follow the road for 400 yards across the flat alluvial land along the Teign, passing Chagford open-air swimming pool on your right. Turn right through Rushford Mill Farm; to the right is a fine set of stepping stones marking a footpath across to the B3206 road by Teign Marsh Farm. Keep left from Rushford Mill Farm and follow the north bank of the river for 1/2 mile. The alders lining the banks become thicker, until you enter a wood proper, largely of oak. Notice the granite sculpture on an island in the river as you head downstream. As you approach Dogmarsh Bridge you have the gardens of the Mill End Hotel on your right.

Cross over the road here and keep heading along the north bank of the river, drawing nearer now to the entrance of the Teign Gorge, below Castle Drogo, high up on its bluff.

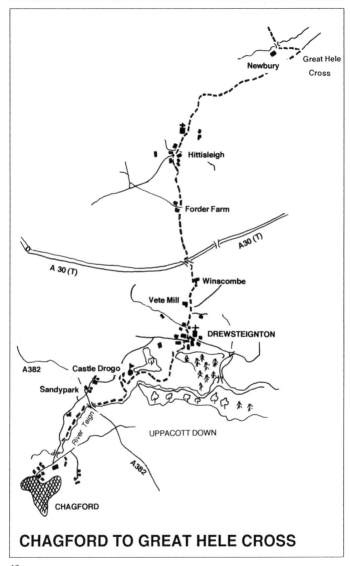

CHAGFORD TO GREAT HELE CROSS

As you enter the woods below Hunter's Tor at a gate and a stile the Two Moors Way turns left, away from the banks of the Teign at last. Ahead is a delightful footpath, the "Fisherman's Path", leading, appropriately enough to the Angler's Arms pub at Fingle Bridge. This is a popular picnic spot - there is a shop here, too. However, the Two Moors Way turns left here, to head north up a little combe towards the thatched dwelling of Gibhouse. You join the tarred drive heading up the combe, soon joined by a second tarred drive. $\frac{1}{2}$ mile after leaving the river the path turns sharply back to the right where the drive exits from the woods. You double back on yourself, the path taking you gently up towards Hunters Tor, through the National Trust Estate of Castle Drogo. As you round the valley side there are superb views down the wooded ravine of the Teign as it makes its way between Uppscott Down and Piddledown Common. Two paths turning off to the left lead you to Castle Drogo itself.

The castle is a modern building, completed in 1930 and therefore one of the last English stately homes. Entirely the work of Edwin Lutyens, it can be visited from Easter to the end of October. If you would like a complete change from walking, and are walking with some friends, you can hire a croquet set for a game on the croquet lawn. There is also of course a tea room and a licensed restaurant. The Two Moors Way keeps along the top of the bluff below the castle itself to the viewpoint of Sharp Tor.

400 yards after Sharp Tor turn left to head due north across Piddledown Common. Suddenly Dartmoor is clear behind and there are very fine views of the dumpy hills of central Devon and beyond them on a clear day the high ground of Exmoor to the north. The delightful foreground to these distant views is of the tower of Holy Trinity church in Drewsteignton. You drop down to the conifers of Rectory Wood and then very steeply down some steps in the trees to

cross a small brook at the end of a farm track; to the right a footpath leads through Drewston Wood to The Anglers Rest pub at Fingle Bridge, back on the River Teign. Head north-east uphill along the embanked lane; it turns sharply to the left and brings you to the village of Drewsteignton. Turn right to walk into the village to the main square by the church. If not overly crowded with car-borne visitors Drewsteignton is delightful to wander around, with some very fine houses. The Drewe Arms pub is famous locally for its venerable landlady and barmaid. There is also a post office stores, next door to the pub.

Leave Drewsteignton down the narrow road to Cheriton Bishop; keep right at Netherton Cross to head down the hill to Vete Mill Cross where you keep left. Turn left off the road at Vete Mill and keep the house on your left. You follow a tiny brook along the east side of the house to find yourself in a sunken walled farm lane hidden from the light by the trees overhead. You emerge from the overhead cover, cross the brook at a muddy patch and follow the lane up the hill to Winscombe Farm. Following the lane through the farm, you climb up the hill to meet the main Cheriton Bishop - Sticklepath road and exit from Dartmoor National Park.

The only hint that you are now out of the National Park is the sudden improvement in the waymarking, with poker-work "Two Moors Way" signs at every turn. Follow the road over the main A30 dual carriageway in its cutting and turn right at the end of the bridge. You pass a modern bungalow on the left, behind a hedge, then turn left to follow a hedge along on your left. You meet a corrugated iron barn athwart the path, then head down the hill towards West Ford. As you near the bottom of the hill you bear slightly to the right across the last field before the trees and enter the oak woods flanking the brook descending from Hole Farm. A narrow path leads you along the bottom of the valley to a farm lane at the River Yeo. You cross the tiny Yeo at a ford with an apparently disused footbridge on the right and head up the hill onto the public road. Take care here; turn right on the road for 30 yards to a right-hand bend; the drive to Forder Cottages turns left. The Two Moors Way turns left off the road here, up a path through a narrow gap in the hedge.

The path takes you straight up the hill, keeping Hill Farm on your left. You cross a thistle-filled field beside the farm, then bear right onto a narrow track. The track almost immediately heads down the hill to the right at a small stand of oaks. Bear left here, down the hill to cross a small brook, then across to the corner of a field to Whitethorn Farm, where you can camp. You join the farm lane running down the hill to cross a small brook, to meet the Whiddon Down road 300 yard short, of Hittisleigh Cross.

Turn right on the road and keep straight ahead at the crossroads, the former school building on your right. There now follows some 3 miles of road walking. Happily this is a very quiet lane. There is a pleasant diversion off this, although it is only signed for those heading south along the Two Moors Way. In fact the diversion offers a slightly longer detour, with a pleasant break from walking along the road, although the net result is yet more road walking! The main road takes you north-east along a ridge between the Yeo valley on the right and the valley of the River Troney down to the left. The diversion is particularly appropriate if you want some shelter from the weather whilst walking along this minor ridge. A mile after Hittisleigh Cross you come to Howard Cross, where a farm lane turns left to Howard Barton. To find the diversion turn left here, then left again off the farm lane at a right-hand bend to head northwards, steeply down the hill into some delightful scattered oak woodland. You meet a tarred lane under the trees (GR735971), just east of a small ford; turn right here to follow the lane back up the hill to

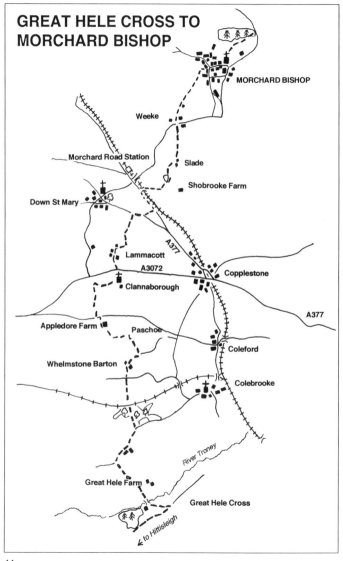

GREAT HELE CROSS TO
MORCHARD BISHOP

MORCHARD BISHOP

Weeke

Morchard Road Station

Slade

Shobrooke Farm

Down St Mary

Lammacott

A3072

Copplestone

Clannaborough

A377

Appledore Farm

Paschoe

Coleford

Whelmstone Barton

Colebrooke

River Troney

Great Hele Farm

Great Hele Cross

← to Hittisleigh

Binneford Cross. $^1/_2$ mile after Binneford Cross you come to Great Hele Cross, where you turn left off the public road, down a farm lane with overhanging oak trees towards Newbury Farm.

You pass the entrance to Great Hele Farm, then turn right just before a gate to cross the River Troney; there used to be a ford here - the old wooden footbridge can still be seen down on the left, now covered in brambles. Turn right off the farm track as it bends to the left (the track not being marked on the map), through a wooden gate and head up the hill. The Way lies up an ancient sunken lane beneath holly and hazel bushes to the right of this rough field, full of broom and tussocks. At the top of the hill you come out of the hedged-in track and head north-west along the track to meet the public road. Turn right on the road and follow it for $^1/_2$ mile past Westcombe Hill Barn on the right. Immediately after the pink-painted Hill Crest bungalow, turn left down a lane into Horwell Wood. The path has been diverted for a short stretch off the forest track; you descend beneath the conifers to cross the Okehampton freight train line at a pair of concrete stiles. The path takes you down to cross the stream with a copse of oak trees on the left, and then uphill along the sunken and muddy Webber's Lane to bring you to Whelmstone Cross, where you go straight ahead towards Whelmstone Barton. There has been a house here since the middle of the thirteenth century; the present house is Tudor and is a fine example of cob and thatch.

The road rises out of a dip just after Whelmstone Barton; as you reach the top of the rise turn left through a gateway with a fine old granite gatepost, showing the series of marks of where it was quarried. Drop down to a small valley with Paschoe House ahead of you and keep to the left of the cottage below it, continuing up the field beside the drive. At Paschoe Farm you keep to the left of the buildings and head directly up the hill behind the sheds with the thick hedge on your right. You reach a gate at the top of the hill and turn right to follow the hedge along on your right towards a small copse of sycamore on the escarpment. Join a farm lane as you enter it and follow it down the hill, keeping right as you exit from the trees. You now walk past Appledore Farm on the right and follow the drive to the public road. Turn left on the road and then immediately right up a ramped entrance to a field to head north towards Sweetfield Farm, with Clannaborough church visible ahead. Head due north from Sweetfield, the signpost on the main road at Clannaborough Cross visible ahead of you. The path turns right to keep parallel to the main road and below it, past Combe Fish Ponds to bring you to the lane to Clannaborough, where you turn left up to the main road.

Clannaborough is first recorded in a charter of 974, during the reign of Ethelred the Unready, as *Cloenesberge* - literally the "cloven hill". It is a strange parish, long and thin, with very few inhabitants near the church. The church is dedicated to the British Celtic saint, Petrock, a dedication commonly found in Cornwall. Its site, on a raised circular platform feature is very unusual and may well point to the spot having pre-Christian religious significance. The present church is almost entirely Tudor, with some rather heavy-handed nineteenth-century restoration. There is a wonderful memorial on the south of the choir, praising all the numerous fine qualities in a victim of drowning in the flooded River Yeo. As is so often the case with remote tiny parishes, there are memorials of those who were killed in the furthest possible "corner of a foreign field" - in this case South Africa and Burma.

Head north up the lane from Clannaborough and turn right on the main road to follow it east for 300 yards to Lammacott Cross. Turn left here to escape the main road and follow the tarred farm road over the hill to turn right at a T-junction just after an old cob barn. There is now a short stretch of walking on a hedged-in green lane, before turning left through a gateway into an arable field with views ahead to Morchard Bishop church on the hill. You follow the hedge along on your left; the farmer happily leaves a wide headland on the edge of his plough here. At the bottom of the field the hedge zigzags around; follow it along the edge of the small wood which you enter at a gate.

Cross the stream and turn right on the road by Barn Shelley, turning off it again after three hundred yards to cross a field of grazing into a second field. You find yourself walking north-east through a very narrow damp paddock with high hedges on either side and little sign of any exit. At the end of this unusual field is a stand of oak trees; beneath them is a stile with a warning sign. Turn left on the verge of the main A377 road and follow it for just sixty yards. Cross the road here and climb a stile to find yourself in a small patch of sedge just before the railway line. Follow the path diagonally to the left and then parallel to the railway line with the fence on your right. You find yourself walking along a narrow fenced-in path inside the line of the old railway fence. This takes you all the way along to Shobrooke Bridge. Turn right here to follow the farm lane up the hill to a cattle grid where you turn left, follow the hedge along to the bottom of the field and then round to the right. This section is not as marked on the map, but is clearly waymarked. You keep the hedge on your left as you cross the next field, Shobrooke Farm at the top of the field on your right. Turn right, along the edge of a small copse and then turn sharp left at the end of it.

Keep the copse on your left and head north to turn right onto the lane to Slade. Make your way up to the house and turn left off the lane into a recent (1990) plantation - the entire field has been planted with trees. This enlightened landowner has planted only native species. A cursory examination reveals oak, rowan, ash, thorn and beech. Keep to the left-hand side of this plantation and leave it over the tiny brook at the far corner. You now head up the hill towards the yellow painted bungalow at Peter's Green, joining a sunken muddy lane taking you up to the road. Turn right and then immediately left along the drive to Woodgate House. Just after Woodgate you reach a crosstracks; keep straight ahead through the elegant iron five bar gate heading north-east along a perfect green lane beneath an oak tree in the hedge. Reaching the end of the lane, the path takes you across two fields, its course marked by two lone oak trees. You reach a spring beneath some bushes and head up the hill on a muddy, hedged-in track, to turn right at the top and walk across several small fields and over a number of stiles to reach the centre of Morchard Bishop at the road junction. Approaching the village, there is a final farewell view of the rounded hills of Dartmoor to the right and behind.

To your right is the London Inn, commemorating the village's position on the old Barnstaple to Exeter (and on to London) main road, now superseded by the A377. The name of the village is one of the few encountered on the walk to have a Celtic origin. The two elements are *mor* - great and *coel* - wood. The said wood has long since disappeared and the name of the village has changed over the years to something resembling the more usual "orchard". The fact that the village occupies a hilltop site would seem to point to the settlement itself having a Celtic, rather than an Anglo-Saxon origin. The manor was at one time held by the Bishop of Exeter, resulting in the suffix. This is very much a village with a heart, with its well-stocked village shop, pub and school. One theory is that the Bishop of Exeter had the church built to give the villagers something to do, rather than poaching his deer!

Climbing north from Ivybridge near the start of the walk
The Huntingdon Warren track above Lud Gate

Looking down the Teign Gorge from below Castle Drogo
Tarr Steps (Walt Unsworth)

DEVON COB AND THATCH

Cob and thatch are as much a part of the Devon scene as scones and clotted cream, and it is along this section of the Way, between the two moors, that most buildings of this type of construction are to be seen. It is the art of building simply using a clayey earth rather as concrete is used in some modern buildings, with the exception that the walls have to be much thicker, and straw is used as an environmentally friendly reinforcement in place of iron rods. The art of building in this way died out in the middle of the nineteenth century as improved transport made the use of other materials more economical. There is an old Devon saying that what cob needs is "a good hat and a good pair of boots". This is a reference to cob's vulnerability to wet. It erodes very rapidly if its top surface is exposed to rain; all cob walls are roofed either with stone, tile or thatch. Equally, damp from below can fatally weaken cob structures. Some cob walls have the first foot or so of their height of granite blocks; others have a "skirting board" effect of a tarred strip along the base. Walls made of cob are generally around 3 feet thick, although some older barns and houses have walls as much as $4^{1}/_{2}$ feet thick. Especially when roofed with thatch, as many are, houses made of cob insulate the interior from the weather to an extent scarcely credible to the inhabitant of a modern house. Owing to the fact that cob uses straw in its construction, it tended not to be used for chimneys. The path of the chimney can be followed by the brickwork up the gable wall in many older cottages.

The base material for cob was always taken from very close to the site of the structure, so its colour changes between one village and the next, varying from a sandy colour to the rich reddish dun colour of Devon soil. Nowadays many cob walls that have a very old core are surfaced with pebbledash and protective white or coloured paint - good preservative but giving a sharp modern veneer to the structure. A form of building with cob, known as "pise", can still be found in the Berber villages of the High Atlas mountains of Morocco; indeed the mighty walls of the Imperial city of Marrakech and the capital of the south, Taroudant, are made of a form of cob, of a similar colour to much of that found in Devon, giving rise to its alternative name of "the red city". Modern pise walls in the High Atlas are built up between shutter boards and the finished wall takes on the layered look, with regular holes where the horizontal poles that held the shuttering in place were removed. None of this can be seen in Devon walls.

Chapter Five
MORCHARD BISHOP TO KNOWSTONE - 19 miles

This is day of dairy farmland, ancient farms and hamlets, with a stretch of relatively painless road walking in the latter part of the day.

Leave Morchard Bishop heading due east along Church Street, towards Black Dog and Woolfardisworthy. Opposite the church turn left at a Two Moors Way marker stone immediately after the village school. The path takes you across an arable field with the hedge on your left and then bears to the right towards Morchard Wood. Entering the wood at a stile it takes you down a woodland ride to Hill Cross, marked on the map with spot height 159.

Turn left along the road and then immediately right at the overgrown entrance to Beech Hill House to head east, down towards the corner of Belkay Copse, the path keeping to the edge of the field beside the wood; follow the concrete post and barbed wire fence along parallel to the edge of the wood, then dropping to cross the infant River Creedy at a footbridge in a line of trees and head up the hill towards the buildings of Brownstone Farm. Make your way around the new farm buildings, keeping them to your right and climb a stile to reach the farm lane. A sign details the bed and breakfast facilities available at the farm. Cross over the road at the end of the farm lane and make your way along a muddy track beneath some trees. You will probably be serenaded by the canine choir from the boarding kennels on your left. Come to the end of a short lane and follow a hedge with a line of beech trees on your right, across two fields.

This point marks the watershed between the catchment of the River Creedy behind you and the River Dalch ahead.

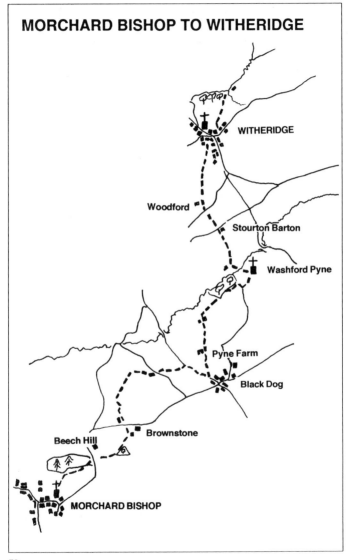

MORCHARD BISHOP TO WITHERIDGE

WITHERIDGE

Woodford

Stourton Barton

Washford Pyne

Pyne Farm

Black Dog

Beech Hill   Brownstone

MORCHARD BISHOP

These two rivers flow into the English Channel and the Bristol Channel respectively. At the end of the second field you turn right through a gate and head down the hill towards the trees, crossing the stream at a footbridge by a ford. Climb the hill among the bracken on the far side to reach the hedge at the top. Do not go through the gate but follow the hedge along on your right to a gate in a dip and then up to the former Wood Farm, now just a dilapidated barn. Follow the old farm lane up the hill and across the fields past a dutch barn to the road. The tower of Witheridge church has come into view over your left shoulder, whereupon you seem to turn away from it. Cross over the road and drop steeply down the hill on a grassy bank, the buildings of Cobscombe Farm (GR797100; it offers bed and breakfast - see Appendix A) in front of you. Follow the farm lane down the hill and turn right into the village of Black Dog. Formerly there were petrol pumps here and a post office stores. Both have now closed, although the pub of the same name is still there, just round the corner on the Puddington Road.

Turn left immediately after the old Post Office and head north down the lane to the fine old cob and thatch of Pyne Farm. Keeping the farm to your left you head along a green lane and then into a field with copious waymarks and steeply down a bank to cross the Sentrys Brook, at a footbridge by a ford. Keep straight ahead, making for the white buildings of Wonham Farm. Keep the buildings of Wonham to your left and turn right immediately after leaving the farm to follow the track along an escarpment and then down a bank to a footbridge into Washford Wood, which you enter at a foot bridge. Take care here; in summer it is almost impossible to see the entrance to the wood and whereas there used to be an obvious ancient route down the slope, this has been ploughed out as the grazing has been improved. You join a track which takes you through the wood, largely of young oaks showing signs of having been coppiced. Turn right at the end of the wood by an old caravan to follow the farm lane to the Washford Pyne road where you turn left and follow it for 300 yards to Washford Pyne. The village is first recorded as *Waseforde* in the Domesday Book. Its name would seem to mean "the ford by the rapids". In 1219 the manor was held by Herbert de Pinu, whose name survives as the second element of the village name. The present church dates from the 1880s and is unusual in having a tiny wooden spire atop the tower. Turn left along a lane beside the church and head steeply down the hill to cross the River Dalch at a footbridge, among some trees, now joining the penultimate map of the Two Moors Way.

Head up the hill to Stourton Barton and follow the farm lane with its poplar trees northwards to the public road, where you find some poultry sheds on the right. Cross the road, and head north-west across two fields, making for Millmoor Farm and its adjacent new bungalow. Cross over the B3042 road here and head northwards up the lane to Woodford, turning right off it as it reaches the farm. The path takes you northwards across two arable fields where the farmer has helpfully left a wide headland to walk on; the tower of St John the Baptist's church in Witheridge is now pleasingly close, straight ahead. As you near the bottom of the hill, a small copse on your right, head diagonally across the field to cross a tiny stream by a footbridge. This is the most helpful of farmers, who each time the field is ploughed, marks the route across the plough with his tractor. You head uphill, the church tower framed in the hedge gaps in front of you.

The final approach into Witheridge is along a cul-de-sac of suburban bungalows, Wiriga Way. You reach the square along a path between the gardens behind the shops on the square. "Wiriga" was the version of Witheridge's name as

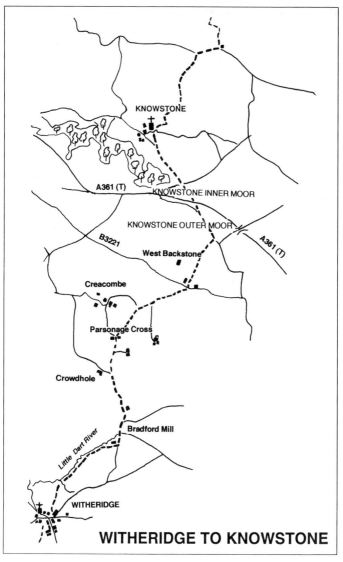

WITHERIDGE TO KNOWSTONE

recorded in the Domesday Book. The name of the village means "ridge with withies" - the use of "withy" as an element in a place name is also found in Withypool, encountered on the following day. If you are following the Way southwards, it is not clearly waymarked from the centre of Witheridge. Make your way to the south side of the square and follow the narrow "No cycling" alleyway beside the shop with the red sign. Witheridge has several shops, including a bakery and two pubs in the centre, the Mitre and the Angel.

From the main square in the village, turn right along the main B3137 Tiverton road. The road forks 200 yards east of the square, a sign pointing to the left to the Parish Hall. Turn left here and after a further 200 yards, turn left again, following the path diverted off a farm lane down the side of a hedge to the left. You descend northwards to Yeo Copse and cross a tributary of the Little Dart River by the ruins of the former East Yeo farm. From here you follow the Little Dart upstream along its southern banks, through Fiddle Copse. For the latter part of this stretch the path lies across a delightfully old-fashioned clayey wet field of cotton grass between Bradford Moor Plantation and the Little Dart River. From this field are fine views of the delightfully situated Bradford Tracey House on the far side of the valley to your left. You join a short lane at the the terrace of houses, Bradford Cottages and turn right on the road.

For the next 6 miles, apart from a break along a muddy track, the Two Moors Way lies all along roads. There simply is no choice for the route. The consolation is that these are by-ways used by few cars, and for much of the route the verges are good and wide, sparing your feet from the hard surface.

Walk northwards down the hill under the trees and cross the river at Bradford Mill, climbing up to fork left after the turning to Bradford Tracey House. The lane runs along the ridge of Creacombe Moor, with occasional fine views through the hedges of the mid-Devon countryside. Turn right at Parsonage Cross and head north-east, the road climbing gently. Bear left as you cross over the B3221 road at the junction by the Old Toll House and find yourself on a muddy track among the trees. Beyond the trees on either side the ground is becoming rougher. As the embanked track nears the road across Knowstone Outer Moor at spot height 263 it becomes increasingly overgrown. Turn left on the unfenced road and follow it down the hill to cross the infant Sturcombe River. The new road swings to the left to the new Knowstone Cross junction on the A361 North Devon link road. Keep right, along the now disused stretch of moorland road to cross the busy and fast main road at a couple of stiles by a low embankment. Walk up the disused stretch on the north side of the main road, across Knowstone Inner Moor, and keep straight ahead at Knowstone Cross. Two thirds of a mile after the cross roads the road bends to the left and dips just after a lay-by on the left-hand side. Turn right here to follow the footpath down the hill, a high hedge on your left and a perfect view of Knowstone church tower ahead of you. The path brings you onto the road almost opposite the thatch-roofed thirteenth-century Masons Arms pub, surely one of the finest on the Two Moors Way and certainly a highlight of this stretch of the walk. Tradition has it that the pub was named after the stonemasons who built St Peter's church who stayed there whilst building it. The landlord welcomes walkers and invites those with tents to camp. The pub also offers accommodation. There is no village shop in Knowstone.

Knowstone is first mentioned in the Domesday Book as *Chenutdestana* and also as *Chenueston*, showing perhaps that the two entries were made by different enquirers. It would seem that the name of the village simply means "Canute's Stone" although we are many miles from the Danelaw and I am not aware of any record of Scandinavian settlement in the area. The name may possibly allude to royal property here, referring to King Canute, ruler of Denmark, Norway and England from 1016 until his death at Shaftesbury in Dorset in 1035. A mile out of the village on the Molland road, on the far side of the Crooked Oak stream is Wadham Farm, birthplace of Sir Nicholas Wadham, whose widow founded Wadham College, Oxford. R.D.Blackmore, the scene of whose most famous novel we walk across on the following day, is supposed to have based the character of Parson Chowne in his little-known novel *The Maid of Sker* on one John Froude, vicar of Knowstone from 1804 to 1853. He was the son of the former incumbent and was born in the village in 1777. A noteworthy son of Knowstone, also the son of the vicar, was John Berry. He, like Horatio Nelson, rose to prominence in the Royal Navy following an upbringing in a remote rural vicarage. Berry distinguished himself in the battle of Sole Bay against the Dutch navy in 1665.

Knowstone is well worth a wander round in the evening; it is possibly the most delightful village on the whole of the Two Moors Way. On sale in the pub is a small book - *Focus on Knowstone* (details in Bibliography) with a wealth of information on the old houses of the village. Arm yourself with it and turn an evening stroll into a fascinating exploration.

Chapter Six
KNOWSTONE TO WITHYPOOL - 12 miles

This is a delightful day's walk, taking you from the rich farming land of central Devon onto the open moorland of Exmoor and ending with a delightful stretch through the ancient woods along the River Barle.

Leaving the Masons Arms, turn left along the road and turn left at Beech Hill Cross down the lane to Owlaborough. You cross the Crooked Oak stream and head up the embanked lane past Owlaborough farm and several farm buildings at intervals along the lane. The surfaced road finishes at a gate and continues as a green lane. On the left is a copse, not marked on the map. Climbing the hill, the lane bends to the right and finishes at a gate in front of a modern barn.

The path continues north-east across the field, following a line of beech trees in the hedge on the right-hand side. The line of trees ends and you turn right through a gate. Keep on the same heading, through another gate to join the lane to Whitefield Farm at the edge of New Moor Plantation.

Turn right onto the road. This is the old Tiverton-Barnstaple main road, formerly the A361. A permissive path was created through the plantation on the south side of the road. Now, with the through traffic using the newer North Devon link road, the road is empty again and it seems likely that the path will become disused. Turn left at the Jubilee Inn and head north along the lane to Bussell's Moor Cross; turn left here and almost immediately right at Highaton Head Cross to walk down to the village of Yeo Mill. There is no pub here, but the Partridge Arms Farm, at one time a coaching inn but now a 200 acre farm, does offer licensed accommodation. There is a post office stores. In the summer of 1993 the bridge

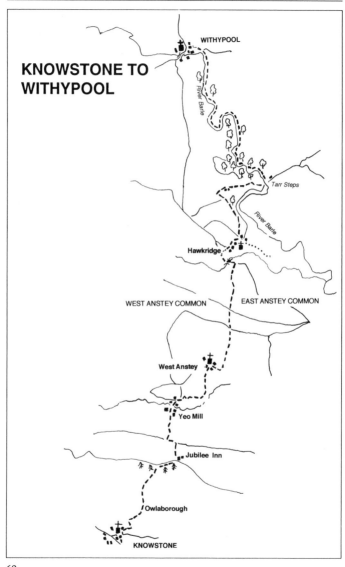

KNOWSTONE TO WITHYPOOL

WITHYPOOL

River Barle

Tarr Steps

River Barle

Hawkridge

WEST ANSTEY COMMON

EAST ANSTEY COMMON

West Anstey

Yeo Mill

Jubilee Inn

Owlaborough

KNOWSTONE

over the Yeo was strengthened and two flood relief culverts constructed on the northern bank - testament to the deterioration of the hydrology of the catchment area with increased field drainage.

Turn right at Yeo Mill Cross, along the lane signed to East Anstey. You cross the West Anstey stream at Wychwood, the road twisting up past Higher Wychwood Farm. 400 yards after the farm, an overgrown track turns off up the hill to the left. Turn left here, up the hill among hazelnut bushes to emerge from the banked lane onto a grazing field with good views. You pass through a gate and walk past the Queen Elizabeth II plantation, planted to commemorate the fortieth anniversary of the accession in 1992. The lane drops to the hamlet of West Anstey. The church of West Anstey is well worth a short diversion; turn left off the road up to the church. Like Clannaborough, a day or so's walk along the Way to the south, it is dedicated to the Celtic St Petrock. Unfortunately, much of the fourteenth- and fifteenth-century building work was lost during restoration in the late nineteenth century. Turn right along the road and follow it over the brow and down to Badlake Farm, then up the hill towards Anstey Common. At Badlake Moor Cross suddenly you leave the tightly hedged fields of mid-Devon behind you and the moorland starts. You now enter Exmoor National Park; there can be few national park boundaries as obvious on the ground as this one, as you make your way from the embanked fields to the open moor.

North of Badlake Moor Cross, the path lies over rough grazing and heather. Head north with a beech hedge on your right; 400 yards beyond Badlake Moor Cross you cross the ridge road and keep heading due north. The walking here is almost level and very easy. Although you are now inside the National Park, you are walking for the most part on the edge of Exmoor proper, with fields of pasture stretching away to the east and bracken and heather, interspersed with clumps of gorse, to the west. Half a mile after crossing the ridge road you come to a gap in the hedge bank to your right. A low wooden signpost here marks the site of Vennford Stone and points your way along the "Two Moors Way - Slade Bridge". This is the watershed between the Bristol Channel and the English Channel, although you are crossing from the Bristol Channel catchment to that of the English Channel - the reverse of what you might expect.

Take care here; turn left off the obvious track to head north-north-west into the gorse, the path well trodden. If you do miss this turning, there is no great problem; you simply give yourself more road walking. You descend across Great Common, looking across to the farm at Zeal. Turn left on the road, steeply down under the trees to Slade Bridge and uphill along Slade Lane between banks. Turn right off the road at a sharp left-hand bend and head across the field, keeping the prominent lone ash tree to your right. During the life span of this tree, either the soil level in the field has dropped by about a yard, or it was originally planted at the top of a hedge-bank, now removed. Turn right along the lane, past the holiday cottages of West Hollowcombe and follow the road into Hawkridge. Turn left at the telephone box opposite a workshop dealing in worked antlers. You pass the post office on the right. This is a simple post office, rather than a post office stores and is actually only open on three half-days a week to serve the pensioners in the village.

There is a very tempting diversion from Hawkridge, heading east along the spur of Hawkridge Ridge, along Row Lane to Brewer's Castle and then following the south bank of the River Barle to meet the road at the bottom of Marchclose Hill. For further details see the excellent walkers' guide *Exmoor and the Quantocks* by John Earle, also published by Cicerone.

Turn right at the post office and head diagonally across the field, now following yellow waymarks, passing through a gate and down to the oak wood of Great Cleeve. You join a track along the uphill side of the wood and cross a clayey, muddy patch below a spring on the hillside. You join the lane to Parsonage Farm at the corner of Row Down Wood and follow it down among the oak trees to cross a tiny stream. The lane takes you up the hill, through the buildings of Parsonage Farm, with red waymarkings to denote a route avoiding the dogs. Immediately after the farm you have the choice of keeping to the top of Parsonage Down, northwards across Withypool Hill to the village of Withypool or descending to Tarr steps.

The Parsonage Down route involves a certain amount of road walking for the latter half, unless you head over the summit of Withypool Hill, which you are entitled to do, even though there is no footpath marked on the map. The better and longer route is to descend to Tarr Steps. Keep heading east, along the spur and then turn right along the edge of a field under a hedge. A gate leads you into a walled track above a wood; follow this down to join the lane to the hotel at Tarr Steps and cross the river at this ancient clapper bridge. As you make your way down through the trees you are close to where Blackmore located the summer residence of the old wise-woman, Mother Meldrum, in Lorna Doone - "...near Hawkridge and close above Tarr Steps".

Tarr Steps is an ancient clapper bridge and well known beauty spot on the River Barle. This is where we meet the Barle; the river is followed intermittently for much of the following day. The name is a derivation of the Anglo-Saxon *Beorgwella*, meaning hill stream. There has always been a certain amount of controversy among historians as to whether Tarr Steps date from the Middle Ages or are prehistoric. Advocates of a prehistoric origin point to the track heading west over Winsford Hill, past the Caratacus Stone, continuing over Molland Common. Both are well supplied with Bronze Age round barrows. Whilst this does indicate the probability of a river crossing here during this period it does not necessarily follow that the bridge structure itself dates from this time. The bridge is a very fine example of a clapper bridge, a type of construction found all over the west country and first passed on the Two Moors Way near Huntingdon Cross, just a few hours walk from Ivybridge. The bridge itself is at the best fording point in the river for some distance; the pool just upstream slows the flow of water before reaching the bridge. There is a lot of evidence to show that there has been deposition in the pool since the bridge was built, so that at the time the bridge was built the usual water level would have been about a foot lower. What is certain is that during the second half of the twentieth century the hydrology of the River Barle catchment was drastically and adversely affected by much of the upland moors being drained, so that rain ran off the moors very quickly, without being absorbed by the "sponge" effect of the peat. In 1941 and 1947 the bridge was damaged by flooding, sections of the spans being carried away on each occasion. This was but a precursor to the catastrophic flood of August 1952, famous for the damage and loss of life it caused in Lynmouth. On this occasion all but one of the spans were carried away and deposited immediately downstream. More dramatically, a car was washed out of the car park (now for disabled drivers only) and carried $2^{1}/_{2}$ miles down the river. In fact the greatest danger to the stone spans is not caused by the water itself but by trees and other debris piling up against the bridge in time of flood. Following the 1952 flood a steel cable was slung across the river just upstream to arrest trees being washed down.

On the far side of Tarr steps the farm serves good food

Walking along the banks of the River Barle (Walt Unsworth)

Withypool Church (Walt Unsworth)

throughout the day and drinks as well. In the summer of 1993 they were offering perhaps the most luxurious of hikers' revivers, glasses of Pimms. Head north along the bank of the River Barle from Tarr Steps, ignoring the private bridge. This is a delightful stretch of the walk, the woods lining the steep valley of the Barle largely of native species. There are patches here of woodland that has never been felled; many of the trees are draped in lichen and ferns.

The river twists and turns through the ancient woodland. After Pit Wood the path seems to keep some distance east from the bank, although there is a sign asking you to keep to the bank itself. You enter Oak Beer Wood a little up the hillside and follow the river upstream, dropping back down to its banks after the wood. For the last stretch before Withypool you are walking along a constructed path below Ham Wood. At the end of the wood you cross two fields and head up the path, twisting steeply up among the trees to reach the Winsford Road as it climbs steeply up out of Withypool.

If you want to walk on to the youth hostel at Exford, turn left down the hill for a short distance on the road, before turning right, up some steps at GR 849356. The path takes you up onto Room Hill and, crossing the B3223 road, runs north to the village of Exford.

Withypool has a small garage, a village shop which shuts at one o'clock on a Saturday and a good pub, the Royal Oak. It is popularly believed that R.D.Blackmore wrote much of *Lorna Doone* whilst staying at the Royal Oak - a letter hanging in the bar referring to this. The name is first mentioned in the Domesday Book; a number of Saxon foresters are named as dwelling here. The name means just what it says, and obviously refers to a pool in the River Barle by which grew

Journey's end - the view down to Lynmouth from Myrtleberry Cleave (photo: Walt Unsworth)·

willows, or "withies". Withypool declined in importance with the creation of the settlement at Simonsbath by the James Boevey and its development under the Knight family, dealt with in the following chapter. Thankfully in summer it remains less crowded than some settlements on and around Devon's moorland as there is no room to park coaches here.

Chapter Seven
WITHYPOOL TO LYNMOUTH - 19 miles

Leaving the Royal Oak in Withypool, turn right and walk along the road for 200 yards to a fork just before the post office stores and garage. Turn right here, along the "no through road" and almost immediately turn right up the hill, past the village hall on your right. You walk uphill across several small paddocks, following the red waymarks until, just over the top of the hill you reach the road. Turn left here and head north-west along Kitridge Lane, a tarred dead-end road finishing at a wooden gate at GR827366.

The track continues with a hedge on your left, crossing Landacre (properly pronounced "Lan'cre") lane. From here to Cow Castle the walking is easy and very pleasant, with obvious, signed paths through the bracken and rough grass and fine views. Three hundred yards west of Landacre Lane the path splits at the head of a small gully leading down to Landacre Bridge. Here the Swainmote Court met twice a year to collect grazing rents and arbitrate in disputes over the Royal Forest; this was until it was moved to Simonsbath by James Boevey for his own ends - see below. A wooden signpost here indicates two routes to Simonsbath - left via Cow Castle, right via Picked Stones. Picked Stones Farm was created on virgin land by John Knight in the early nineteenth century - see below. Keep left at the junction, the track contouring and then descending towards the River Barle.

As you descend towards the pine plantation on the north bank of the river there are fine views back to the left to Landacre Bridge and up the valley of the Sherdon Water. At the confluence of the two rivers is a popular spot for families to park their cars and enjoy the river. You go through a gate

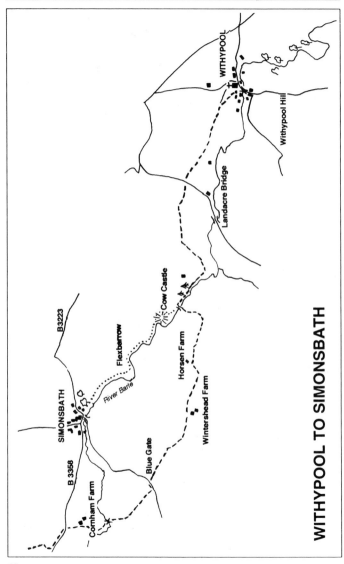

WITHYPOOL TO SIMONSBATH

in a high banked hedge, then to follow a track towards the coniferous plantation. This banked hedge is part of the wall built by the Knight family in 1824 to enclose their estate, effectively the former Royal Forest. You are now at last in the Exmoor Forest. Shortly before the wood the track joins the river; the banks of the Barle here are delightful, especially in late summer when the orange blooms of the montbretia hang over the clear waters of the Barle. The Way heads along a good track through the bottom of the plantation, three small streams crossing it in the trees. The Two Moors Way proper crosses the river here by the footbridge just upstream of the ford and follows the Horsen stream past the rock outcrop of Great Ferny Ball, joining the lane to Horsen Farm, past Wintershead Farm and north-west up to the road junction at Blue Gate.

It may well be that you want to head along the river to the village of Simonsbath; in so doing you will commit yourself to two miles of road walking on the far side of the village. A visit to Simonsbath is recommended, not only to refuel the body, but to put the history of Exmoor into perspective. There is no village shop in Simonsbath where you can buy supplies to eat later, but there is the Exmoor Forest Hotel (where you can camp) and Boevey's teashop - the origin of the name is explained below, in the section on the Knights of Exmoor.

The route along the valley to Simonsbath has a great deal of interest, as well as the prospect of refreshment at the end of it. Crossing the White Water at its confluence with the River Barle, you pass the rock outcrop of The Calf on your right (not as the map shows) and then the Iron Age fortification of Cow Castle. Unfortunately the trees of Pickedstones Plantation obscure the impression of the strategic siting of the fort as you approach it upstream; it is well worth climbing to the summit. There is nothing bovine in its name; "Cow" is derived from the Celtic "Caer". Further on, the path is delightful, passing over a miniature saddle between Flexbarrow and Winstitchen Hill. Flexbarrow is not a barrow, but a natural hill; the first element of the name is derived from *fleot* , stream, referring to the River Barle. You pass the ruins of Wheal Eliza cottage and mine - "Wheal" being the usual name for a mine in Cornwall. This was an unsuccessful attempt at iron extraction by the Knight family and is explained more fully below. You enter Simonsbath by the nature reserve of Birchcleave Woods - a fine beech wood sheltering the village. The short cut back to the Way from Simonsbath is to climb up the steep hill on the B3223 road to Lynton, turning left after 2 miles along the permissive path heading west, upstream along the infant river Exe, bringing you to Exe Head, where you pick up the directions below.

From the junction at Blue Gate (GR758376) turn left and walk for 300 yards along the road and turn right through a gate. The path lies north-west, a well defined track across the moor. It descends to a tributary of the River Barle and becomes deeply gullied, testament to the heavy storms that sweep across Exmoor from the Bristol Channel. As you descend the Burcombe Valley to cross the Barle you are once again on a good track. You cross the river at Cornham Ford, a footbridge supplementing the original ford. Nowadays this is a lonely spot.

In the middle of the nineteenth century this was the scene of much activity as Frederic Knight persuaded the Dowlais mining company of Wales that sufficient iron ore was to be found here and at Blue Gate, just passed, to make for an economically viable mine. Work was even started on an ore-carrying railway to take the ore over Brendon Common to be shipped from Porlock Weir; this however was never completed. The arrangement was made between Knight and the Dowlais company in 1855; by 1858 the company had seen

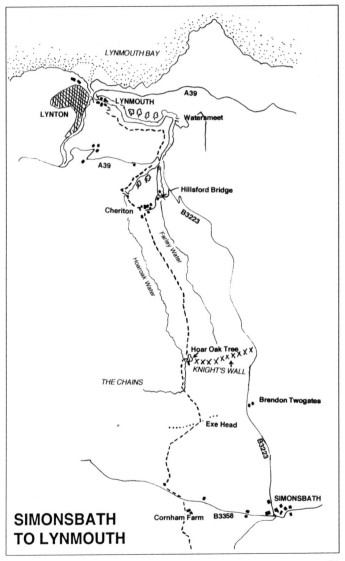

SIMONSBATH TO LYNMOUTH

almost no return on its investment and ceased operations. Knight resorted once more to litigation and won his case, the company paying him £7,000 to release itself from its contract with Knight.

Follow the track up the hill to the in-fields around Cornham Farm. The farm was founded by the Knight family in 1828; the spot is recorded as being *Quarnam* in 1656 and is a reference to the *cwrn*, the rocky outcrops by the River Barle. There is a fine view to the left upstream along the Barle - a pleasant farewell to this fairest of Exmoor's rivers. In the days of the Cornham Ford mine the miners took this route up the valley to the Acland Arms inn, built expressly for them, but strategically placed 2 miles' walk west of the mine itself. Head due north across the fields around Cornham Farm, keeping to the left of the buildings. From the scene of one of Knight's failures, here is an example of his success, the farm still today much as he laid it out. Suddenly the landscape is a lot tamer as you walk down the farm drive. At the end of the drive there is a sign, pointing north towards Titchcombe and Exe Head, indicating a right of way. However there is nothing yet marked on the OS map and the path is not well defined. It does, however, save a stretch on the road, where the traffic moves quite fast.

Turn left at the end of Cornham Farm drive to follow the B3358 Exford-Challacombe road north-west over the top of the hill. Here you are once again on an ancient trackway, this one being an early English one. It is the Harepath - literally the "army path". This was a route running from the Midlands, south to Gloucester and Bristol, from there over the Quantocks and then the Brendon Hills, just to the east of Exmoor. From Exford it ran along the line of the present day B3358 road west via Simonsbath. Two thirds of a mile beyond the point where the Two Moors Way turns off the road it turned left (at GR733400) to cross the Barle and head south-west on its way to Mole's Chamber and on to Barnstaple via Bratton Fleming. It is unusual to find an Anglo-Saxon route that keeps to the high ground as this one does; it is generally believed that it was a route used for the English levies to move west to support the harassing of the Celtic population in their retreat into Cornwall. The section between the main road and Mole's Chamber is one of the few stretches where it is still visible as an ancient trackway.

Turn right off the main road at GR743399, the point marked by some sheep sheds on the right-hand side. Immediately after the sheep sheds the path becomes merely faint wheel ruts bearing to the right across the sheep-grazed turf. If you keep heading exactly due north, parallel to the fence to your right and 150 yards east of it, you will reach the waymarked gate. Head north from this gate across the field to bring you to a second gate at the far corner of the field. This is at the head of the Titchcombe stream, GR744409.

East from this gate runs a line of trees; make your way diagonally across the field of rough grazing, heading north-west for 1/2 mile to bring you to the gates at Exe Head. You are now on the moor proper, leaving John Knight's reclaimed farmland behind. Once again you are on the watershed between the Bristol Channel and the English Channel, leaving that of the English Channel behind you. Turn left through the gate in the fence to your left and head north along a rutted track across the moor from the tiny runnel that is the infant River Exe. At GR750420 you meet a signpost. On the map the Two Moors Way is written as heading northwards, along the western flank of Exe Plain. In fact the path proper drops down as a prominent track, into the valley of the Hoar Oak Water, to cross it at its confluence with the stream running down Long Chains combe at the ruin of a cottage.

From here the path runs north along the west bank of the Hoar Oak Water. The famous Hoar Oak, marked and named on the map, is still little more than a sapling; it was planted in 1917, replacing one dating from 1662. The name has nothing to do with frost, but derives from *har*, Anglo-Saxon for boundary. The 1662 replanting was by James Boevey; not only did the oak mark the boundary of the Royal Forest (hence its name) but was a gesture of support for Charles II who had hidden in an oak tree and in honour of whom a multitude of pubs were named "The Royal Oak". The fact that the beech trees just below seem to be flourishing, in contrast to the struggling oak, is a fine illustration of the fact that beech grows higher up and further north than oak.

Cross the Hoar Oak Water here by the footbridge and head up the hill by the Hoar Oak itself, turning left to pass through a gate in the hedge-bank. This marks the county boundary; henceforward the Two Moors Way lies all in Devon. The wall itself is also the boundary of Exmoor Forest and is thus three boundaries - county, parish and Royal forest. It was built on the orders of John Knight to enclose his estate. Having entered the Knight's estates by Landacre Bridge you are now leaving them; go through a gate in the wall and head diagonally up the hill. The path is not well defined up onto Cheriton Ridge; it continues uphill, due north, whilst the river, lined with trees, swings to the north west towards Hoar Oak Farm. Once on the top of the ridge you join a well marked track heading over Cheriton Ridge, with fine views to the right, across to Brendon Common and the B3223 road from Simonsbath to Hillsford Bridge. This is also part of the Tarka Trail, a figure-of eight route of 180 miles established by the local authority to commemorate Henry Williamson's fictitious otter. A guidebook for this path is available in bookshops in the area.

As you approach the scattered houses of the hamlet of Cheriton, bear just to the right, so that you are walking just on the eastern side of the top of Cheriton. You leave the moor along a walled lane, through a gate. Joining the tarred road, turn left at the road junction and follow this narrow lane past a farm, round a sharp left bend, and past a new bungalow on the left. The road deteriorates to a track and heads very steeply down the hill to Smallcombe Bridge, by a cottage. Immediately over the bridge turn right and head north through the woods of Combe Park. This is a permissive path by courtesy of the National Trust; before 1992 the Two Moors Way followed the road from Cheriton to Hillsford Bridge. Soon you approach the back of the smart Combe Park Hotel, set in a clearing in the woods in the narrow valley of the Hoar Oak Water.

You join the drive of the hotel and walk down the valley to Hillsford Bridge, where the A39 coast road meets the confluence of the Farley Water and Hoar Oak Water, before following the valley down to the well-known beauty spot of Watersmeet. With the thick woods, ferns and rhododendrons, there is an air of the Himalayas here.

Turn left on the main road at the hairpin bend and head up the hill to a left-hand hairpin bend. Turn right off the road here, along a green path through oak woods. The air of wildness is utterly dispelled as the landscape takes on a well-tended parkland air. You leave the woods by an iron-age fort and head north above the woods. This final stretch of The Two Moors Way is movingly beautiful, especially if walked in the early morning or the evening. Far below you to your right, the East Lyn River burbles its way towards the sea. The sentinel tower of Countisbury church is visible on the hillside behind Foreland Point. I have never walked this stretch without the evocative accompaniment of buzzards wheeling over the gorge, the air full of their mewing cries. Occasionally a raven glides past, with its rich croaking cry. Few long distance paths can have as dramatic a finale as this, with the hills of Wales looming across the far side of the Bristol

Channel.

Half a mile after leaving the main road, a path is signed to your right, down to Watersmeet - a very steep drop through the bracken and into the woods. The path swings to the west, following the top of Myrtleberry Cleave, the anthills here a favourite haunt of green woodpeckers. At Myrtleberry Hangings the path zig-zags down the hillside to cross a gully under the trees and then zig-zags back up to reach the top of the escarpment by the green lane and footpath leading to West Lyn. At long last you reach the crags of Oxen Tor; if you are walking round to the youth hostel at Lynbridge, keep left here, to follow the path across Summer House Hill to cross the West Lyn River at a footbridge just upstream of the hostel.

From Oxen Tor the path plunges down into the oak woods and joins a track. Finally, as the track goes round a hairpin bend to the right the path heads into a sort of tunnel of vegetation between two high stone walls. It becomes a tarred footpath, passes between several cottages advertising the comforts of their bed and breakfast arrangements and finally reaches its end by a marker stone opposite the church. Your transition from the wild grandeur of Exmoor to the frippery of Lynmouth is marked by the model railway exhibition opposite the path's end. Turn left along the pavement to cross the road down into Lynmouth itself.

Lynmouth is a shock after the glorious isolation of the moors. Unless you are there early in the morning or out of season there are crowds thronging the tiny port. It is a fine reward for the tired and hungry hiker to feast on cream teas or a pub lunch before contemplating the next move.

WARDENS OF THE FOREST AND THE KNIGHTS OF EXMOOR

In the past Exmoor Forest was part of the Royal Demesne in much the same way that the New Forest was, or indeed

Richmond Park. The term "Forest" was an administrative one and did not imply that Exmoor was during historical times under tree cover. With the unifying of the minor English Kingdoms into one in the tenth century the unclaimed lands of England gradually became to be regarded as Royal property. This was enshrined at the time of the Norman Conquest, the king's powers on the Exmoor being exercised by the Warden of the Forest.

This system changed radically under the financial reforms of Henry Tudor, victor of the Battle of Bosworth in 1485. Henry VII recognised that the key to founding a secure dynasty was to build up his exchequer, which he did most successfully. In 1508 he leased the Forest itself from the Crown, so that all the Crown's former rights and grazing rents came to be held by the lessee for the duration of the lease - an early example of what we now know as "privatization", except that the current fashion seems to be for the government to sell assets, rather than merely lease them. The next English Revolution, in the middle of the seventeenth century, saw a further dramatic change in Exmoor's fortunes. In 1649, a few months after the beheading of Charles I, the Rump of Parliament passed an act permitting the sale of the Royal property. (Parallels may be drawn with the disposal of the former state assets in the countries of eastern Europe following the revolutions of 1989.)

Exmoor was bought by a wealthy Midlander of Dutch extraction, one James Boevey. Perhaps the most important point to make about the whole transaction is that it is recorded that there was no one dwelling within the boundaries of the former Royal Forest that Boevey had bought. It was as though he had bought a kind of English Siberia in miniature. Having bought the lands Boevey immediately moved here and built what is known as the "first house in the Forest", at the ancient track crossing at Simonsbath. The house,

Simonsbath Lodge, is still there, though it has been much altered since his day. He is commemorated by Boevey's Tea House - recommended for a spot of hiker's feasting. If the commoners of the area had hoped for an easier time, freed of the burden of the Royal yoke, they were to be disappointed as Boevey attempted to turn the forest into his personal empire.

With the Restoration of Charles I's son, Charles II, in 1660 all former crown lands sold eleven years before were repossessed; Boevey simply bought the lease of the Forest so that he enjoyed the rights of the Warden enshrined in 1508. Exmoor was scarcely any less his private empire, as he had the right to exclude justices of the peace and sheriffs from entering within the boundary of the forest. In effect he was very nearly the absolute ruler of Exmoor. From 1672 to 1674 Boevey was imprisoned in The Hague; when he returned he embarked on a wildly ambitious law case to prove that the Wardenship of the Forest included all the adjoining common lands *outside* the clearly-defined forest boundaries. In 1679 he lost this case, and, perhaps fearing for his safety should he continue to live in the area he settled in Cheam in Surrey.

Exmoor continued under less rapacious Wardens through the seventeenth century, latterly under the Acland dynasty, commemorated today by the farm at GR732396, and formerly by the Acland Arms inn nearby. The next period of change for Exmoor may be seen as a consequence of the whirlwind in Europe arising out of the French Revolution of 1789. The victory at Trafalgar in 1805 and Napoleon's invasion of Spain in 1808 involved Britain in massive naval expansion as French land conquests were countered by an attempt at blockade by sea. Suddenly wood was an essential strategic material for shipbuilding, of which Britain was short. The government instigated attempts to use crown lands as forests and a resulting survey of Exmoor recommended that the lands be divided up, with an amount made over to the Warden, Sir Thomas Acland, to compensate him for the loss of his lease of the entire forest.

This was duly done and Acland was awarded one third of the former Royal Forest. In 1818 however, it was decided that Exmoor was not suitable for timber-growing after all and the King's Commissioner of Woods and Forests decided that the crown lands should be sold freehold. They were bought by a certain John Knight of Worcestershire, who proceeded to buy Acland's third as well as a small amount belonging to Sir Charles Bamfylde, so that he owned all former Royal Forest.

Knight was an energetic and learned man; his vision was to apply some of the new agricultural methods being developed at Holkham in Norfolk by Thomas Coke. He embarked on a plan of reclaiming the moor by heather-burning and ploughing, augmented by road building, the present day roads from Simonsbath largely being built by him. He built several farms, among them Cornham, passed by the Two Moors Way, where hitherto there had been just barren moor. He introduced Cheviot sheep to the moor, still seen today. Knight retired from his efforts in 1841 without having reaped the harvest of his efforts. His son Frederic continued his work, but still his tenant farms showed no profit. Knight attempted to recoup his losses by sinking iron mines at Wheal Eliza, Cornham Ford and Blue Gate (see above), following the examples on the nearby Brendon Hills. This, too was unsuccessful. It was popular for a time to scorn the efforts of the Knights of Exmoor, but by the time of the death of Frederic Knight in 1897, his farms were viable, as indeed they are today. Sadly his only son, Frederic Winn had predeceased him and the Knight line died.

The estates were sold to the Fortescue family who were already Devon landowners. They are commemorated by a modern cairn beside the road up to Blue Gate from

Simonsbath. There is a connection with the later stretch of the walk, for Sir John Fortescue, an eminent figure, librarian at Windsor Castle and author of a sixteen volume *History of the British Army*, assisted Henry Williamson with the introduction to the first, private, edition of *Tarka the Otter* (a highly recommended read - see Bibliography). The final few steps on Exmoor coincide with the route of the modern Tarka Trail.

Appendix A
ACCOMMODATION

BED AND BREAKFAST

The recommended way to walk the Two Moors Way is by staying farmhouse bed and breakfast; you learn far more about the region by staying in its farming households than by gazing at the nylon walls of your tent. It is also pleasant to help the local economy without the deadening effect on local communities of long-term stays in holiday cottages.

The list below does not imply any recommendation by the author, unless mentioned in the text. Establishments are listed according to the order passed, starting the Two Moors Way at Ivybridge. Accommodation can often be found between the night halts implied in the text. These are listed under the settlement where the day starts. No attempt has been made to quote prices: in general, the more expensive establishments are listed first, which means hotels, followed by bed and breakfast establishments. Where the house offering bed and breakfast is not in an obvious village on the map, in general it is located with a grid reference. Many of the establishments listed below are on the Two Moors Way itself - those that are are identfied with a @. In 1993 farmhouse bed and breakfast cost around £12-15 per head. Most of the establishments listed below offer an evening meal; an asterisk (*)after the address indicates that an evening meal is not available.

Whatever time of year you walk the Two Moors Way, you should telephone ahead to arrange your bed and breakfast. This need not be overly restricting if instead of planning every day stage you telephone a day or two ahead as you walk. It must be admitted that there is great pleasure in seeing a bed and breakfast sign outside a picturesque farm that takes your fancy and enjoying the pleasure of discovery.

Ivybridge

Sunny Side Hotel, Weston Road, Ivybridge
0752 892561

Mr & Mrs Hancox, The Toll House, Exeter Road, Ivybridge
0752 893522

White Oaks Farm, Davey's Cross, Filham, Ivbridge
0752 892340

Mrs P Salter, Strashleigh Farm, Ivybridge PL21 9JP
0752 892226

Hillhead Farm, Ugborough, Ivybridge (GR674563)
0752 892674

Ven Farm, Ugborough, Ivybridge (GR685566)
0364 73240

Scorriton and Holne

Massie Dinning, The Barn, Scorriton, Buckfastleigh
03643 491

Mrs J Bellows, Mardlewood House, Higher Combe, Scorriton
03643 152

Newcombe Farm, Scorriton 03643 734

Church House Inn, Holne, Ashburton 03643 208

Mrs R Parsons, Higher Michelcombe Farm, Holne, Ashburton
03643 483

Wellpritton Farm, Holne, Ashburton 03643 273

Mrs A Haycraft, Middle Leat Farm, Holne, Ashburton
03643 413

Mrs J Henderson, Dodbrooke Farm, Holne, Ashburton
03643 461

Mrs P Adnitt, Chast Gate Farm, Holne, Ashburton
03643 261

Mrs W Bevan, Church House Inn, Holne, Ashburton
03643 208

Mrs A Mortimore, Hazelwood, Holne, Ashburton TQ13 7SJ
03643 235

Mrs A Walker, Courts Close, Holne, Ashburton
03643 291

Poundsgate, Newton Abbot and area

Leusdon Lodge Hotel, Poundsgate, Newton Abbot
TQ13 7PE @ 03643 304/573, Fax 599

New Cott Farm, Poundsgate 03643 421

Maggie and Jan Baty, Townwood Fm, Poundsgate (GR717720) @
03643 310

Mrs Partridge, Leigh Tor Farm, Poundsgate (GR709718)
03643 374

Mrs Brown, Lower Aish, Poundsgate 03643 304

Ponsworthy

Mrs E Fursdon, Old Walls Farm, Ponswothy, Newton Abbot
03643 222

Widecombe in the Moor

Sheena Tower, Widecombe in the Moor 03642 308

Mrs P Boyes, Rutherford House, Widecombe in the Moor
03642 264

Heather Bank, Widecombe in the Moor 03642 205

Mrs B Hicks, Higher Venton Farm, Widecombe in the Moor
(GR722760) 03642 235

Mrs D Nosworthy, Lower Southway Farm, Widecombe in
the Moor 03542 277

Chagford, Newton Abbot and area

Mrs H Stanbury, Teigncombe Farm, Chagford, Newton Abbot
(GR672872) @ 0647 433410

Mrs M Malseed, Frenchbeer Farm, Chagford (GR6785)
0647 432427

Gidleigh Park Hotel, Chagford (GR678880) 0647 432225

Mill End Hotel, Sandypark, Chagford (GR713893) @
0647 432282

Easton Court Hotel, Easton Cross, Chagford 0647 433469

Mr E Willett, Glendarah House, Chagford 0647 433270

Bly House Hotel, Chagford 0647 432404

Three Crowns Hotel, High St, Chagford 0647 433444

Mrs E Harvey, Devonia, 19 Lower St, Chagford 0647 433344

Mrs E Law, Lawn House, ChagforD 0647 433329

Mrs May, Claremont, 13 Mill St, Chagford 0647 433304
St Johns West, Murchington, Chagford (GR689888)
   0647 432468

Drewsteignton
Mrs C Harrison, Hunts Tor House, Drewsteignton 0647 21228
Ford House, Drewsteignton 0647 21243
Mrs L Emanuel, The Old Rectory, Drewsteignton 0647 21269
The Old Inn Restaurant, The Square, Drewsteignton
   0647 21276
Mrs A Bowden, Bowbeer Farm, Drewsteignton
   0647 21239

Hittisleigh
Mrs L Hopton, Bowacre Farm, Hittisleigh * 0647 24366
Mrs R Lloyd, Whitethorn Farm, Hittisleigh 0647 24273
Mrs C Evans, East Church Farm, Hittisleigh 0647 24366

Colebrook
Mrs P Hill, Birchmans Farm, Colebrook, Crediton
   0363 82393
Mrs D Hockridge, Butsford Farm, Coleford, Crediton
   0363 84353
Mrs R Bowyer, Hillerton Barton, Bow * 0363 82501

Morchard Bishop
Mrs D Snell,Shippens, Polson Hill, Morchard Bishop 0363 877424
Mrs G Warren, Arcadia, Chumleigh Road, Morchard Bishop
   0363 877210
Beech Nut, Beech Hill, Morchard Bishop 0363 877228
Mrs M Tapp, Harries Cottage, The Green, Morchard Bishop
   0363 877459
Arjay's Fishing Retreat, Oldborough (GR775061)
   0363 877437

Black Dog, Crediton
Mrs Wedlake, Brownstone Farm, Black Dog, Crediton (GR796095)
   @   0363 877256

Mrs C Crang, Wonham Farm, Black Dog (GR803110) @
0884 860221
Mrs G Gillbard, Hele Barton, Black Dog 0884 860278
Mrs M Crang, Sentrys, Black Dog 0884 860288
Mrs C Ayres, Cobscombe Farm, Black Dog (GR797 010) @
0884 860075

Witheridge, Tiverton
The Angel Inn, Witheridge, Tiverton 0884 860429
The Mitre Inn, Witheridge 0884 860395
Mrs M Child, Hope House, 6 The Square, Witheridge
0884 860012
Mr R Woolacott, West Yeo Farm, Witheridge (GR801151)
0884 860300
Mrs A Webber, Marchweeks Farm, Thelbridge (GR796115)
0884 860418
Thelbridge Cross Inn, Thelbridge (GR790120) 0884 860316

Knowstone, South Molton
The Masons Arms Inn, Knowstone, South Molton EX36 4RY
03984 231/582
(Recommended)
Mrs L Jones, The Old Chapel, Knowstone 03984 404
Mrs Bray, West Bowden Fm, Knowstone EX36 4RP (GR834224)
03984 224

West Anstey, South Molton
The Jubilee Inn, West Anstey, South Molton (GR844250) @
03984 401
Mrs H Milton, Partridge Arms Farm, Yeo Mill (GR842262) @
03984 217
Mrs V Witney, Bridge House, Yeo Mill, West Anstey *
03984 385
Lady Loram, The Old Vicarage, West Anstey, South Molton @
03984 529
Mrs E Burton, The Church House, West Anstey, South Molton
03984 247

Hawkridge
Mrs R Branfield, East Hollowcombe Farm, Hawkridge
  03984 338

Tarr Steps: The Tarr Steps Hotel, Hawkridge @ 064385 293

Withypool, Somerset
Westerclose Country House, Withypool, Somerset TA24 7QR
  064383 302
Mrs M Bennett, Fir Tree Cottage, Withypool, Somerset
  064383 453
Mrs B Clatworthy, The Old Rectory, Withypool, Somerset
  064383 553

Simonsbath, Somerset
The Exmoor Forest Hotel, Simonsbath, Somerset TA24 7SH
  064383 341
Mrs L Pile, Moorland Cottage, Simonsbath   064383 458
Mrs A Brown, Emmetts Grange Farm, Simonsbath (GR753369)
  064383 282
Mrs Derben, Wintershead Farm, Simonsbath (GR771368)
  064383 222
Mrs T Hawkins, Gallon House, Simonsbath, TA24 7JT
  064383 283

Cheriton: J Young, South Cheriton Farm, Lynton, North Devon
  0598 55280

Lynmouth, North Devon
The Tors Hotel, Lynmouth EX35 6NA 0598 53236
Bath Hotel, Harbourside, Lynmouth EX35 6EL 0598 52238
The Beacon Hotel, Lynmouth EX35 6ND 0598 53268
Orchard House Hotel, Watersmeet Road, Lynmouth EX35 6EP
  0598 53247
Mrs Francis,Glenville House, 2 Tors Road, Lynmouth EX35 6ET
  0598 52202
Mrs B Pile, Oakleigh, 4 Tors Road, Lynmouth EX35 6ET
  0598 52220

Mrs A Hawkins, Tregonwell Guest Hse, Tors Road, Lynmouth
0598 53369
Mrs B Watts, Rocklyn, Tors Road, Lynmouth EX35 6ET
0598 52233

Lynton, North Devon
Rockvale Hotel, off Lee Road, Lynton, North Devon EX35 6HW
0598 52279/53343
Sandrock Hotel (Mr & Mrs Harrison), Longmead, Lynton
0598 53307
Sylvia House Hotel, Lydiate Lane, Lynton EX35 6HE
0598 52391
Southcliffe Hotel, Lee Road, Lynton EX35 6BT 0598 53328
Longmead House Hotel, Longmead, Lynton. EX35 6DQ
0598 52523
Mayfair Hotel, Lynway, Lynton 0598 53227
Northcliff Hotel, North Walk, Lynton 0598 52357
Woodlands Hotel, Lynbridge, Lynton 0598 52324

YOUTH HOSTELS

There are three youth hostels which are useful to walkers along the
Two Moors Way. These are Bellever (0882 88221), Exford (064383
288) and Lynbridge (0598 52327). Sadly the hostel at Gidleigh has
shut. Prices range from £4 to £12 (1993 prices). In common with
many youth hostels in the country, facilities have lately been
improved, with small, multi-bedded rooms. You need to be a
member of the YHA to stay, but you can join at any of the hostels.

The Youth Hostel Association, South England Regional Office,
11b York Road
Salisbury, Wilts SP2 7AP
0722 337515, Fax 0722 414027

or South West Regional Office,
Belmont Place, Stoke
Plymouth, Devon.
0752 52753

CAMPING

Whilst walking on the open access land of Dartmoor it is permitted for the self-contained backpacker to camp wild, so long as he or she is discreet and leaves no evidence of ever having been there.

Away from these areas there are enough campsites so that the dedicated tent-dweller can camp on every night of the Two Moors Way. The list below is laid out in order of walking, starting in Ivybridge.

White Oaks Farm, Davey's Cross, Filham, Ivbridge
  0752 892340

Massie Dinning, The Barn, Scorriton, Buckfastleigh
  03643 491
Mrs J Henderson, Dodbrooke Farm, Holne, Ashburton
  03643 461
Mrs A Mortimore, Hazelwood, Holne, Ashburton TQ13 7SJ
  03643 235
Mr D Powell, Holne Court Farm, Ashburton
  03643 271

Mrs Brown, Lower Aish Camping Site, Poundsgate (GR706722)
  03643 229
Mrs Nosworthy, Lower Southway Farm, Widecombe in the Moor
  (GR724767) 03542 277
Cockingford Bridge Campsite (GR716751)

Barley Meadow Campsite, Crockernwell (GR744924)
  0647 21629
Mrs R Lloyd, Whitethorn Farm, Hittisleigh @ (GR734946)
  0647 24273
Mr W Weston, West Wotton Farm, Colebrooke
  0363 82293

A Smith, Middlecott Farm, Morchard Bishop
  03637 474
Mrs G Warren, Arcadia, Chumleigh Road, Morchard Bishop
  0363 877210

Beech Nut, Beech Hill, Morchard Bishop
   0363 877228

Mrs Wedlake, Brownstone Farm, Black Dog
   0363 877256
Mr R Fausset, Pyne Farm, Black Dog
   0884 869699
J Hayes, Wodford Farm, Witheridge, Tiverton
   0884 860345
Mr P Turner, West Backstone Farm, Rackenford
   0884 488341
The Masons Arms Inn, Knowstone, South Molton EX36 4RY
   03984 231/582
Mrs Millman, Eastercott Farm, East Knowstone, South Molton
   03984 215
Mrs H Milton, Partridge Arms Farm, Yeo Mill (GR842262)
   03984 217
Mrs Robbins, Dunsley Farm, West Anstey, South Molton
   03984 246
Mrs E Eden Badlake Farm, West Anstey, South Molton
   03984 303
R Connell, Tarr Farm, Tarr Steps, Dulverton
   064383 383

Exmoor Forest Hotel, Simonsbath
   064383 341

Mrs G Layton, Sunny Lyn Caravan Park, Lynbridge
   0598 53384
Mr Bowen, Chancellor View Caravan Park, West Lyn
   0598 53349

Appendix B
USEFUL ADDRESSES AND TELEPHONE NUMBERS

Exmoor National Park Information Office, The Esplanade, Lynmouth
0598 52509

Lynton Information Office, The Town Hall, Lynton
0598 52225

Exeter Tourist Information Office, Civic Centre, Paris Street, Exeter
0392 265700

British Rail, Exeter
0392 433551

Red Bus Company, Barnstaple (operates Lynton-Barnstaple buses)
0271 45444

Devon Bus Enquiry Line, Barnstaple
0271 382800

Tourist Information Office, Barnstaple
0271 388583

The Dartmoor Tourist Association, 8 Fitzford Cottages, Tavistock, Devon PL19 8BD

The Dartmoor Preservation Association, Crossings Cottage, Dousland, Devon PL20 6LU 0822 8928

Dartmoor National Park Headquarters, Parke, Haytor Road, Bovey Tracey TQ13 9JQ 0626 832903

Select Bibliography
BACKGROUND READING

John Earle, *Exmoor and the Quantocks - A Walker's Guide*, Cicerone Press 1991. An excellent book of day walks in the area.

John Earle, *Walking on Dartmoor*, Cicerone Press 1987. Many of his excellently researched day walks on Dartmoor coincide with the route of the Two Moors Way. Very highly recommended.

Michael Dunn, *Walking Ancient Trackways*, David and Charles 1986. There are good sections on a part of the Mariners Way, a part of the Abbott's Way, as well as a number of relatively short ancient trackways all over the country.

Verna Rapley, *Focus on Knowstone*, published by the author 1990. This can be bought at the excellent Masons Arms pub in the village of Knowstone. It is a wonderful companion for a stroll around Knowstone, one of the finest villages on the Two Moors Way.

R.D.Blackmore, *Lorna Doone*, (first publ. 1869) Pan Classics. A very fine holiday novel on Exmoor folk, set in the era of the Charles II and then the Monmouth rebellion. The archetypal story, so beloved by Hollywood, of a beautiful girl brought up among robbers and thieves who turns out to be the heiress to a fortune, stolen at a tender age. None of which dulls her affection for her lusty suitor, Jan Ridd. It is a fine portrait of lawless times and the utter remoteness of seventeenth-century Exmoor - not quite a "rattling good tale", more "pleasantly rumbling".

Henry Williamson, *Tarka the Otter*, Penguin. Worth reading again, even if you read it as a child.

REFERENCE

Eilert Ekwall, *The Concise Oxford Dictionary of English Place Names*.
S.H.Burton, *Devon Villages*, Robert Hale 1973
W.G.Hoskins, *Devon*, David & Charles 1954

S.H.Burton, *The Lorna Doone Trail*, Exmoor Press

S.H.Burton, *Exmoor*, Robert Hale 1969 and 1974. Useful background on Exmoor - now out of print but often available in libraries.

Jacquetta Hawkes, *Guide to Prehistoric and Roman Monuments in England and Wales*

Sir Nikolaus Pevsner, *Buildings of England*, published by Penguin. Within this series the volumes on South Devon, North Devon, South & West Somerset.

J.H.B.Peel, *Portrait of Exmoor*, Robert Hale

S.H.Burton, *The North Devon Coast*, Werner Laurie

Michael Harrison, *The Story of Tarr Steps*, privately published, on sale at Tarr Steps Farm

Dr Sweetapple-Horlock, *Guide to Tarr Steps*, published 1928

Victor Bonham Carter, *Essence of Exmoor*, Exmoor Press

Roger Burton, *Heritage of Exmoor*, published by the author, available from 12 Style Close, Rumsam, Barnstaple, Devon EX32 9EL

William Crossing, *Guide to Dartmoor*, Peninsula. A reprint of the 1925 edition and no less authoritative now than it was then. Other Crossing guides to specific aspects of Dartmoor are available as reprints.

CICERONE GUIDES

Cicerone publish a wide range of reliable guides to walking and climbing abroad

FRANCE
TOUR OF MONT BLANC
CHAMONIX MONT BLANC - A Walking Guide
TOUR OF THE OISANS: GR54
WALKING THE FRENCH ALPS: GR5
THE CORSICAN HIGH LEVEL ROUTE: GR20
THE WAY OF ST JAMES: GR65
THE PYRENEAN TRAIL: GR10
THE RLS (Stevenson) TRAIL
TOUR OF THE QUEYRAS
ROCK CLIMBS IN THE VERDON
WALKS IN VOLCANO COUNTRY (Auvergne)
WALKING THE FRENCH GORGES (Provence)
FRENCH ROCK

FRANCE / SPAIN
WALKS AND CLIMBS IN THE PYRENEES
ROCK CLIMBS IN THE PYRENEES

SPAIN
WALKS & CLIMBS IN THE PICOS DE EUROPA
WALKING IN MALLORCA
BIRDWATCHING IN MALLORCA
COSTA BLANCA CLIMBS
ANDALUSIAN ROCK CLIMBS
THE WAY OF ST JAMES

FRANCE / SWITZERLAND
THE JURA - Walking the High Route and
    Winter Ski Traverses
CHAMONIX TO ZERMATT The Walker's
    Haute Route

SWITZERLAND
WALKING IN THE BERNESE ALPS
CENTRAL SWITZERLAND
WALKS IN THE ENGADINE
WALKING IN TICINO
THE VALAIS - A Walking Guide
THE ALPINE PASS ROUTE

GERMANY / AUSTRIA / EASTERN EUROPE
THE KALKALPEN TRAVERSE
KLETTERSTEIG - Scrambles
WALKING IN THE BLACK FOREST
MOUNTAIN WALKING IN AUSTRIA
WALKING IN THE HARZ MOUNTAINS
WALKING IN THE SALZKAMMERGUT
KING LUDWIG WAY
HUT-TO-HUT IN THE STUBAI ALPS
THE HIGH TATRAS

ITALY & SLOVENIA
ALTA VIA - High Level Walks in the Dolomites
VIA FERRATA - Scrambles in the Dolomites
ITALIAN ROCK - Rock Climbs in Northern Italy
CLASSIC CLIMBS IN THE DOLOMITES
WALKING IN THE DOLOMITES
THE JULIAN ALPS

MEDITERRANEAN COUNTRIES
THE MOUNTAINS OF GREECE
CRETE: Off the beaten track
TREKS & CLIMBS IN WADI RUM, JORDAN
THE ATLAS MOUNTAINS
WALKS & CLIMBS IN THE ALA DAG (Turkey)

OTHER COUNTRIES
ADVENTURE TREKS - W. N. AMERICA
ADVENTURE TREKS - NEPAL
ANNAPURNA TREKKERS GUIDE
CLASSIC TRAMPS IN NEW ZEALAND
TREKKING IN THE CAUCAUSUS

GENERAL OUTDOOR BOOKS
THE HILL WALKERS MANUAL
FIRST AID FOR HILLWALKERS
MOUNTAIN WEATHER
MOUNTAINEERING LITERATURE
THE ADVENTURE ALTERNATIVE
MODERN ALPINE CLIMBING
ROPE TECHNIQUES IN MOUNTAINEERING
MODERN SNOW & ICE TECHNIQUES
LIMESTONE -100 BEST CLIMBS IN BRITAIN

CANOEING
SNOWDONIA WILD WATER, SEA & SURF
WILDWATER CANOEING
CANOEIST'S GUIDE TO THE NORTH EAST

CARTOON BOOKS
ON FOOT & FINGER
ON MORE FEET & FINGERS
LAUGHS ALONG THE PENNINE WAY

*Also a full range of guidebooks
to walking, scrambling, ice-climbing,
rock climbing, and other adventurous
pursuits in Britain and abroad*

*Other guides are constantly being added to the Cicerone List.
Available from bookshops, outdoor equipment shops or direct (send for price list)
from CICERONE, 2 POLICE SQUARE, MILNTHORPE, CUMBRIA, LA7 7PY*

CICERONE GUIDES

Cicerone publish a wide range of reliable guides to walking and climbing in Britain, and other general interest books.

LAKE DISTRICT - General Books
A DREAM OF EDEN
LAKELAND VILLAGES
LAKELAND TOWNS
REFLECTIONS ON THE LAKES
OUR CUMBRIA
THE HIGH FELLS OF LAKELAND
CONISTON COPPER A History
LAKELAND - A taste to remember (Recipes)
THE LOST RESORT? (Morecambe)
CHRONICLES OF MILNTHORPE
LOST LANCASHIRE (Furness area)
THE PRIORY OF CARTMEL

LAKE DISTRICT - Guide Books
CASTLES IN CUMBRIA
THE CUMBRIA CYCLE WAY
WESTMORLAND HERITAGE WALK
IN SEARCH OF WESTMORLAND
CONISTON COPPER MINES Field Guide
SCRAMBLES IN THE LAKE DISTRICT
MORE SCRAMBLES IN THE LAKE DISTRICT
SHORT WALKS - SOUTH LAKELAND
WINTER CLIMBS IN THE LAKE DISTRICT
WALKS IN SILVERDALE/ARNSIDE
BIRDS OF MORECAMBE BAY
THE EDEN WAY
WALKING ROUND THE LAKES

NORTHERN ENGLAND (outside the Lakes
BIRDWATCHING ON MERSEYSIDE
CANAL WALKS Vol 1 North
CANOEISTS GUIDE TO THE NORTH EAST
THE CLEVELAND WAY & MISSING LINK
THE DALES WAY
DOUGLAS VALLEY WAY
HADRIANS WALL Vol 1 The Wall Walk
HERITAGE TRAILS IN NW ENGLAND
THE ISLE OF MAN COASTAL PATH
IVORY TOWERS & DRESSED STONES (Follies)
THE LANCASTER CANAL
LANCASTER CANAL WALKS
LAUGHS ALONG THE PENNINE WAY
A NORTHERN COAST-TO-COAST
NORTH YORK MOORS Walks
THE REIVERS WAY (Northumberland)
THE RIBBLE WAY
ROCK CLIMBS LANCASHIRE & NW
THE YORKSHIRE DALES A walker's guide
WALKING IN THE SOUTH PENNINES
WALKING IN THE NORTH PENNINES
WALKS IN THE YORKSHIRE DALES (3 VOL)
WALKS IN LANCASHIRE WITCH COUNTRY
WALKS IN THE NORTH YORK MOORS
WALKS TO YORKSHIRE WATERFALLS (2 vol)
WALKS ON THE WEST PENNINE MOORS
WALKING NORTHERN RAILWAYS (2 vol)
WALKING IN THE WOLDS

DERBYSHIRE & EAST MIDLANDS
WHITE PEAK WALKS - 2 Vols
HIGH PEAK WALKS
WHITE PEAK WAY
KINDER LOG
THE VIKING WAY
THE DEVIL'S MILL / WHISTLING CLOUGH (Novels)

WALES & WEST MIDLANDS
THE RIDGES OF SNOWDONIA
HILLWALKING IN SNOWDONIA
HILL WALKING IN WALES (2 Vols)
ASCENT OF SNOWDON
WELSH WINTER CLIMBS
SNOWDONIA WHITE WATER SEA & SURF
SCRAMBLES IN SNOWDONIA
SARN HELEN Walking Roman Road
ROCK CLIMBS IN WEST MIDLANDS
THE SHROPSHIRE HILLS A Walker's Guide
HEREFORD & THE WYE VALLEY A Walker's Guide
THE WYE VALLEY WALK

SOUTH & SOUTH WEST ENGLAND
COTSWOLD WAY
EXMOOR & THE QUANTOCKS
THE KENNET & AVON WALK
THE SOUTHERN-COAST-TO-COAST
SOUTH DOWNS WAY & DOWNS LINK
SOUTH WEST WAY - 2 Vol
WALKING IN THE CHILTERNS
WALKING ON DARTMOOR
WALKERS GUIDE TO DARTMOOR PUBS
WALKS IN KENT
THE WEALDWAY & VANGUARD WAY

SCOTLAND
THE BORDER COUNTRY - WALKERS GUIDE
SCRAMBLES IN LOCHABER
SCRAMBLES IN SKYE
THE ISLAND OF RHUM
CAIRNGORMS WINTER CLIMBS
THE CAIRNGORM GLENS (Mountainbike Guide)
THE ATHOLL GLENS (Mountainbike Guide)
WINTER CLIMBS BEN NEVIS & GLENCOE
SCOTTISH RAILWAY WALKS
TORRIDON A Walker's Guide
SKI TOURING IN SCOTLAND

REGIONAL BOOKS UK & IRELAND
THE MOUNTAINS OF ENGLAND & WALES
    VOL 1 WALES VOL 2 ENGLAND
THE MOUNTAINS OF IRELAND
THE ALTERNATIVE PENNINE WAY
THE PACKHORSE BRIDGES OF ENGLAND
THE RELATIVE HILLS OF BRITAIN
LIMESTONE - 100 BEST CLIMBS

Also a full range of EUROPEAN and OVERSEAS guidebooks - walking, long distance trails, scrambling, ice-climbing, rock climbing.

Other guides are constantly being added to the Cicerone List.
Available from bookshops, outdoor equipment shops or direct (send s.a.e. for price list) from
CICERONE, 2 POLICE SQUARE, MILNTHORPE, CUMBRIA, LA7 7PY

Printed by CARNMOR PRINT & DESIGN
95-97 LONDON ROAD, PRESTON, LANCASHIRE, UK.